Third Workshop on Fact Extraction and VERification (FEVER 2020)

Online
9 July 2020

ISBN: 978-1-7138-1385-9

Printed from e-media with permission by:

Curran Associates, Inc.
57 Morehouse Lane
Red Hook, NY 12571

Some format issues inherent in the e-media version may also appear in this print version.

Printed with permission by Curran Associates, Inc. (2020)

For permission requests, please contact the Association for Computational Linguistics at the address below.

Association for Computational Linguistics
209 N. Eighth Street
Stroudsburg, Pennsylvania 18360

Phone: 1-570-476-8006
Fax: 1-570-476-0860

acl@aclweb.org

Additional copies of this publication are available from:

Curran Associates, Inc.
57 Morehouse Lane
Red Hook, NY 12571 USA
Phone: 845-758-0400
Fax: 845-758-2633
Email: curran@proceedings.com
Web: www.proceedings.com

ACL 2020

FEVER

Fact Extraction and VERification

Proceedings of the Third Workshop

July 9, 2020

We thank our sponsor Amazon for their generous support.

Introduction

With billions of individual pages on the web providing information on almost every conceivable topic, we should have the ability to collect facts that answer almost every conceivable question. However, only a small fraction of this information is contained in structured sources (Wikidata, Freebase, etc.) – we are therefore limited by our ability to transform free-form text to structured knowledge. There is, however, another problem that has become the focus of a lot of recent research and media coverage: false information coming from unreliable sources.

To ensure accuracy, this content must be verified. However, the volume of information precludes human moderators from doing so. It is paramount to research automated means to verify accuracy and consistency of information published online and the downstream systems (such as Question Answering,Search and Digital Personal Assistants) which rely on it. The FEVER series of workshops has been a venue for ongoing research in this area.

Organizers:

Christos Christodoulopoulos (Amazon)
James Thorne (University of Cambridge)
Andreas Vlachos (University of Cambridge)
Oana Cocarascu (Imperial College London)
Arpit Mittal (Amazon)

Invited Speakers:

Isabelle Augenstein (University of Copenhagen)
Jon Roozenbeek (University of Cambridge)
Noam Slonim (IBM)
Philip Resnik (University of Maryland)
Dilek Hakkani-Tur (Amazon)

Program Committee:

Isabelle Augenstein (University of Copenhagen) Tuhin Chakrabarty (Columbia University) Diego Esteves (University of Bonn) Ivan Habernal (UKP Lab, Technische Universität Darmstadt) Andreas Hanselowski (UKP lab, Technische Universität Darmstadt) Alexandre Klementiev (Amazon) Nayeon Lee (Hong Kong University of Science and Technology) Pranava Swaroop Madhyastha (University of Sheffield) Christopher Malon (NEC Laboratories America) Marie-Francine Moens (KU Leuven) Yixin Nie (UNC) Farhad Nooralahzadeh (University of Oslo) Wolfgang Otto (GESIS – Leibniz-Institute for the Social Sciences in Cologne) Ankur Padia (University of Maryland, Baltimore County) Tamara Polajnar (University of Cambridge) Laura Rimell (DeepMind) Jodi Schneider (UIUC) Diarmuid Ó Séaghdha (Apple) Kevin Small (Amazon) Motoki Taniguchi (Fuji Xerox) Paolo Torroni (Alma Mater - Università di Bologna) Zeerak Waseem (University of Sheffield)

Table of Contents

Conference Program

Please note that the FEVER 2020 Workshop will be held virtually. The exact times and links to each presentation can be found at https://fever.ai

9th July

Opening Remarks
FEVER Organizers

Project Debater
Noam Slonim

Towards explainable fact checking
Isabelle Augenstein

Oral presentations

Simple Compounded-Label Training for Fact Extraction and Verification
Yixin Nie, Lisa Bauer and Mohit Bansal

Stance Prediction and Claim Verification: An Arabic Perspective
Jude Khouja

How to "inoculate" people against misinformation and online extremism
Jon Roozenbeek

Beyond Facts: The Problem of Framing in Assessing What is True
Phil Resnik

Poster Session

A Probabilistic Model with Commonsense Constraints for Pattern-based Temporal Fact Extraction
Yang Zhou, Tong Zhao and Meng Jiang

Developing a How-to Tip Machine Comprehension Dataset and its Evaluation in Machine Comprehension by BERT
Tengyang Chen, Hongyu Li, Miho Kasamatsu, Takehito Utsuro and Yasuhide Kawada

Language Models as Fact Checkers?
Nayeon Lee, Belinda Li, Sinong Wang, Wen-tau Yih, Hao Ma and Madian Khabsa

Maintaining Quality in FEVER Annotation
Leon Derczynski, Julie Binau and Henri Schulte

Distilling the Evidence to Augment Fact Verification Models
Beatrice Portelli, Jason Zhao, Tal Schuster, Giuseppe Serra and Enrico Santus

Integration of (Un)structured World Knowledge In Task Oriented Conversations
Dilek Hakkani-Tur

Closing Remarks
FEVER Organizers

Simple Compounded-Label Training for Fact Extraction and Verification

Yixin Nie* **Lisa Bauer*** **Mohit Bansal**
UNC Chapel Hill
{yixin1, lbauer6, mbansal}@cs.unc.edu

Abstract

Automatic fact checking is an important task motivated by the need for detecting and preventing the spread of misinformation across the web. The recently released FEVER challenge provides a benchmark task that assesses systems' capability for both the retrieval of required evidence and the identification of authentic claims. Previous approaches share a similar pipeline training paradigm that decomposes the task into three subtasks, with each component built and trained separately. Although achieving acceptable scores, these methods induce difficulty for practical application development due to unnecessary complexity and expensive computation. In this paper, we explore the potential of simplifying the system design and reducing training computation by proposing a joint training setup in which a single sequence matching model is trained with compounded labels that give supervision for both sentence selection and claim verification subtasks, eliminating the duplicate computation that occurs when models are designed and trained separately. Empirical results on FEVER indicate that our method: (1) outperforms the typical multi-task learning approach, and (2) gets comparable results to top performing systems with a much simpler training setup and less training computation (in terms of the amount of data consumed and the number of model parameters), facilitating future works on the automatic fact checking task and its practical usage.

1 Introduction

The increasing concern with the spread of misinformation has motivated research regarding automatic fact checking datasets and systems (Pomerleau and Rao, 2017; Hanselowski et al., 2018a; Bast et al., 2017; Pérez-Rosas et al., 2018; Zhou et al., 2019; Vlachos and Riedel, 2014; Wang, 2017; Shu et al., 2019a,b). The Fact Extraction and VERification (FEVER) dataset (Thorne et al., 2018a) is the most recent large-scale dataset that enables the development of data-driven neural approaches to the automatic fact checking task. Additionally, the FEVER Shared Task (Thorne et al., 2018b) introduced a benchmark, the first of this kind, that is capable of evaluating both evidence retrieval and claim verification.

Several top-ranked approaches on FEVER (Nie et al., 2019a; Yoneda et al., 2018; Hanselowski et al., 2018b) decompose the task into 3 subtasks: document retrieval, sentence selection, and claim verification, and follow a similar pipeline training setup where sub-components are developed and trained sequentially. Although achieving higher scores on benchmarks, pipeline training is time-consuming and imposes difficulty for fast application development since downstream training relies on data provided by a fully-converged upstream component. The impossibility of parallelization also causes data-inefficiency as training the same input sentence for both sentence selection and claim verification requires twice the computation, whereas humans can learn the task of sentence selection and claim verification jointly.

In this work, we simplify the training procedure and increase training efficiency for sentence selection and claim verification by merging redundant components and computation that exist when training the two tasks separately. We propose a joint training setup in which sentence selection and claim verification are tackled by a single neural sequence matching model. This model is trained with a *compounded label space* in which for a given claim, an input sentence that is labeled as "NON-SELECT" for sentence selection module training will also be labeled as "NOTENOUGHINFO" for claim verification module training. Similarly, input evidence that is labeled as "SUPPORTS" or

Our code will be publicly available on our webpage.

* Equal contribution

Proceedings of the Third Workshop on Fact Extraction and VERification (FEVER), pages 1–7
July 9, 2020.

"REFUTES" for claim verification module training will also be labeled as "SELECT" for sentence selection module training.

To validate our new setup, we compare with the previous pipeline setup and a multi-task learning setup which trains the two tasks alternately. Fig. 1 illustrates differences among these three setups.

Results indicate that: our method (1) outperforms the multi-task learning setup, and (2) yields comparable results with a top performing pipeline-trained system while consuming less than half the number of data points, reducing the parameter size by one-third, and converging to a functional state much faster than the pipeline-trained system. We argue that the aforementioned design simplification and training acceleration are valuable especially during time-sensitive application development.

2 Related Work

2.1 Previous FEVER Systems

Many of the top performing FEVER 1.0 systems, all achieving greater than 60% FEVER score on the respective leaderboard (Nie et al., 2019a; Yoneda et al., 2018; Hanselowski et al., 2018b), share the same pipeline training schema in which document retrieval, sentence selection, and claim verification are all trained separately.

While Nie et al. (2019a) proposed formalizing sentence selection and claim verification as a similar problem, sentence selection and claim verification are still trained separately on the task, which contrasts with our setup. Additionally, Yin and Roth (2018) proposed a hierarchical neural model to tackle both sentence selection and claim verification at the same time, but did not induce computational savings as in our setup.

2.2 Information Retrieval

Neural networks have been successfully applied to information retrieval tasks in Natural Language Processing (Huang et al., 2013; Guo et al., 2016; Mitra et al., 2017; Dehghani et al., 2017; Qi et al., 2019; Nie et al., 2019b) with a focus on relevant retrieval. Information retrieval is generally a relevance-matching task whereas claim verification is a more semantics-intensive task. We consider using a single semantics-focused model to conduct both sentence retrieval and claim verification.

2.3 Natural Language Inference

Natural Language Inference (NLI) requires a system to classify the logical relationship between two sentences in which one is the premise and one is the hypothesis. This classifier decides whether the relationship is entailment, contradiction, or neutral. Several large-scale datasets have been created for this purpose, including the Stanford Natural Language Inference Corpus (Bowman et al., 2015) and the Multi-Genre Natural Language Inference Corpus (Williams et al., 2018). This task can be formalized as a semantic sequence matching task, which bears resemblance to both the sentence retrieval and claim verification tasks.

2.4 Multi-Task Learning

Multi-task learning (MTL) (Caruana, 1997) has been successfully used to merge Natural Language Processing tasks (Luong et al., 2016; Hashimoto et al., 2017; Dong et al., 2015) for improved performance. Parameter sharing, in particular sharing of certain structures such as label spaces, has been used widely in several NLP tasks for this purpose (Liu et al., 2017; Søgaard and Goldberg, 2016). Zhao et al. (2018) used a multi-task learning setup for FEVER that shared certain layers between sentence selection and claim verification modules. Augenstein et al. (2018) used shared label spaces in MTL for sequence classification. Following this work, Augenstein et al. (2019) used shared label spaces for automatic fact checking. However, the labels involved in this work were limited to claim verification labels only, and did not incorporate sentence selection as we do in this paper.

2.5 Fake News Detection

In addition to the FEVER shared task, other recent work in fake news detection has focused on several aspects of data collection and statement verification. Shu et al. (2019b) looked into the role of social context in fake news detection. Additionally, Shu et al. (2019a) also explored creating explainable fake news detection.

3 Model

3.1 Sequence Matching Model

Sentence selection and claim verification can be easily structured as the same sequence matching problem in which the input is a pair of textual sequences and the output is a semantic relationship label for the pair. Nie et al. (2019a) proposed using

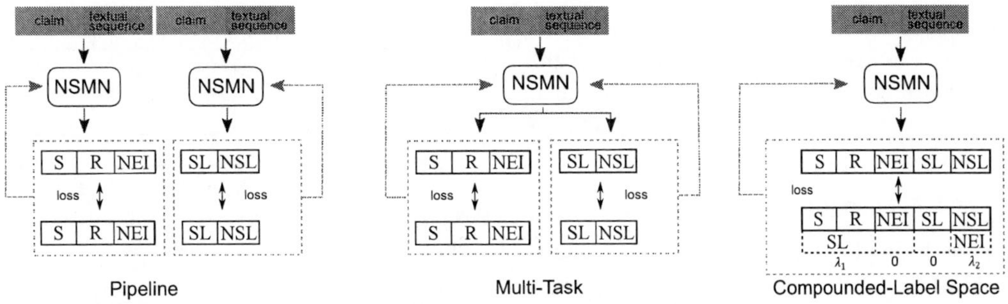

Figure 1: Different training setups. In the pipeline setup, sentence selection and claim verification models are trained separately. In the multi-task setup, the two tasks are treated separately, but use a single model. In the compounded-label training setup, the training is simplified to a single task by mixing the data of the two tasks and allowing controlled supervision between the two tasks. S, R, NEI, SL, and NSL represent "SUPPORTS", "REFUTES", "NOTENOUGHINFO", "SELECT", and "NON-SELECT", respectively.

the same architecture, the neural semantic matching network (NSMN), on the two tasks and showed it was effective on both. Thus, we use the same NSMN model with a modified output layer in our experiments.

3.2 Neural Semantic Matching Network (NSMN)

For convenience, we give a description similar to the original paper (Nie et al., 2019a) about the model below.

Encoding Layer:

$$\bar{\mathbf{U}} = \text{BiLSTM}_e(\mathbf{U}) \in \mathbb{R}^{d_1 \times n} \tag{1}$$

$$\bar{\mathbf{H}} = \text{BiLSTM}_e(\mathbf{H}) \in \mathbb{R}^{d_1 \times m} \tag{2}$$

where $\mathbf{U} \in \mathbb{R}^{d_0 \times n}$ and $\mathbf{H} \in \mathbb{R}^{d_0 \times m}$ are the two input sequences, d_0 and d_1 are input and output dimensions, and n and m are lengths of the two sequences.

Alignment Layer:

$$\mathbf{A} = \bar{\mathbf{U}}^\top \bar{\mathbf{H}} \in \mathbb{R}^{n \times m} \tag{3}$$

where an element in $\mathbf{A}_{[i,j]}$ indicates the alignment score between i-th token in $\mathbf{U}$ and j-th token in $\mathbf{H}$. Aligned sequences are computed as:

$$\tilde{\mathbf{U}} = \bar{\mathbf{H}} \cdot \text{Softmax}_{\text{col}}(\mathbf{A}^\top) \in \mathbb{R}^{d_1 \times n} \tag{4}$$

$$\tilde{\mathbf{H}} = \bar{\mathbf{U}} \cdot \text{Softmax}_{\text{col}}(\mathbf{A}) \in \mathbb{R}^{d_1 \times m} \tag{5}$$

where $\text{Softmax}_{\text{col}}$ is column-wise softmax, $\tilde{\mathbf{U}}$ is the aligned representation from $\bar{\mathbf{H}}$ to $\bar{\mathbf{U}}$ and vice versa for $\tilde{\mathbf{H}}$. The aligned and encoded representations are combined as:

$$\mathbf{F} = f([\bar{\mathbf{U}}, \tilde{\mathbf{U}}, \bar{\mathbf{U}} - \tilde{\mathbf{U}}, \bar{\mathbf{U}} \circ \tilde{\mathbf{U}}]) \in \mathbb{R}^{d_2 \times n} \tag{6}$$

$$\mathbf{G} = f([\bar{\mathbf{H}}, \tilde{\mathbf{H}}, \bar{\mathbf{H}} - \tilde{\mathbf{H}}, \bar{\mathbf{H}} \circ \tilde{\mathbf{H}}]) \in \mathbb{R}^{d_2 \times m} \tag{7}$$

where f is one fully-connected layer with a rectifier as an activation function and $\circ$ denotes element-wise multiplication.

Matching Layer:

$$\mathbf{R} = \text{BiLSTM}_m([\mathbf{F}, \mathbf{U}^*]) \in \mathbb{R}^{d_3 \times n} \tag{8}$$

$$\mathbf{S} = \text{BiLSTM}_m([\mathbf{G}, \mathbf{H}^*]) \in \mathbb{R}^{d_3 \times m} \tag{9}$$

where $\mathbf{U}^*$ and $\mathbf{H}^*$ are sub-channels of the input $\mathbf{U}$ and $\mathbf{H}$ without GloVe, provided to the matching layer via a shortcut connection.

Output Layer:

$$\mathbf{r} = \text{Maxpool}_{\text{row}}(\mathbf{R}) \in \mathbb{R}^{d_3} \tag{10}$$

$$\mathbf{s} = \text{Maxpool}_{\text{row}}(\mathbf{S}) \in \mathbb{R}^{d_3} \tag{11}$$

$$h(\mathbf{r}, \mathbf{s}, |\mathbf{r} - \mathbf{s}|, \mathbf{r} \circ \mathbf{s}) = \mathbf{m} \tag{12}$$

where function h denotes two fully-connected layers with a rectifier being applied on the output of the first layer.

3.3 Compounded-Label Output Layer

We propose the following compounded-label output layer for simpler, more efficient training. Given the input pair x_i, the NSMN model is:

$$\mathbf{m} = \text{NSMN}(x_i) \tag{13}$$

where $\mathbf{m} \in \mathbb{R}^4$ is the output vector of NSMN in which the first three elements correspond to claim verification and the last element to sentence selection. Then, the probabilities are calculated as:

$$\mathbf{y}_{cv} = \text{softmax}(\mathbf{m}_{[0:3]}) \tag{14}$$

$$y_{ss} = \text{sigmoid}(m_3) \tag{15}$$

where $\mathbf{m}_{[0:3]}$ denotes the first three elements of $\mathbf{m}$ and $\mathbf{y}_{cv} \in \mathbb{R}^3$ denotes the probability of predicting the relation between the input and claim as "SUPPORTS", "REFUTES", or

"NOTENOUGHINFO", while m_3 denotes the fourth element of $\mathbf{m}$ and $y_{ss} \in \mathbb{R}$ indicates the probability of choosing the input as evidence for the claim. This allows us to transfer the model's outputs to predictions in a compact way.

3.4 Compounded-Label Training

In order to simplify the training procedure and increase data efficiency, we introduce compounded-label training. Consider the model output vector:

$$\hat{\mathbf{y}}_i = \left[\begin{array}{c} \mathbf{y}_{cv} \\ \hline y_{ss} \\ 1 - y_{ss} \end{array}\right] \tag{16}$$

where $\hat{\mathbf{y}}_i \in \mathbb{R}^5$ is the concatenation of $\mathbf{y}_{cv}$ and $[y_{ss}, 1 - y_{ss}]^\top$. To optimize the model, we use the entropy objective function:

$$\mathcal{J} = -\mathbf{y}_i \cdot \log(\hat{\mathbf{y}}_i) \tag{17}$$

In a typical classification setup, the ground truth label embedding y_i is a one-hot column vector chosen from an identity matrix, where the dimension equals the total number of categories. However, our compounded-label embedding is structured as the matrix with some supervision provided in the zero-area of one-hot embeddings shown below:

$$\begin{bmatrix} 1 & 0 & 0 & 0 & 0 \\ 0 & 1 & 0 & 0 & 0 \\ 0 & 0 & 1 & 0 & \lambda_2 \\ \lambda_1 & \lambda_1 & 0 & 1 & 0 \\ 0 & 0 & 0 & 0 & 1 \end{bmatrix} \tag{18}$$

The first 3 columns are label embeddings for "SUPPORTS", "REFUTES", and "NOTENOUGHINFO" in verification and the last 2 columns are the label embeddings for "SELECT" and "NON-SELECT" in sentence selection, resp. Thus, for a given claim, "SUPPORTS" and "REFUTES" evidence will also give supervision as positive examples to sentence selection weighted by λ_1 and "NON-SELECT" sentences will also give supervision as "NOTENOUGHINFO" evidence to claim verification weighted by λ_2.

4 Experimental Setup

We focused on comparing the following five NSMN[1] training setups for sentence selection and claim verification. We obtain upstream document retrieval data using the method in Nie et al. (2019a). Training details are in the appendix.

[1]We remove the external WordNet features from NSMN for simplicity and speed.

	Pip.	Mul.	Mix.	Cmp.
Shared Parameters	✗	✓	✓	✓
Mix. in Same Batch	✗	✗	✓	✓
Supv. for Other Task	✗	✗	✗	✓

Table 1: Properties of different training setups. "**Pip.**", "**Mtl.**", "**Mix.**", "**Cmp.**" stand for pipeline, multi-task learning, direct mixing, and compounded-label training setup, respectively. 'Supv.'=Supervision.

Model	FEVER Score	Rec.	# Param	Data
D.M.	57.92	85.3	18.2M	11.5M
MTL.	62.25	85.3	18.2M	14.4M
Rdc-Pip.	61.82	83.7	18.2M	11.4M
C.L.	64.68	86.6	18.2M	3.52M
Pip.	65.37	86.8	27.6M	9.6M

Table 2: Final performance, evidence recall, model size, and data consumption (until convergence) for all 5 setups. We measure data consumption as the amount of data the model used for parameter updating, e.g., 10K updates w/ batch size 32 consumes 320K data. 'D.M.'=direct mixing, 'C.L.'=compounded-label, 'MTL.'=multi-task learning, 'Rdc-Pip.'=pipeline w/ reduced size, 'Pip.'=pipeline (Nie et al., 2019a).

Pipeline: We train separate sentence selection and claim verification models as in Nie et al. (2019a).

Multi-task Learning: We follow the neural multi-task learning setup called alternate training (Dong et al., 2015; Luong et al., 2016; Hashimoto et al., 2017), where each batch contains examples from a single task only. We build a single NSMN model for both selection and verification and alternatively optimize the two tasks.

Direct Mixing: We simply blend the input examples of the two tasks into the same batch, providing additional simplicity over our multi-task learning setup in which batches need to be task-exclusive.

Compounded-Label Training: We also blend the inputs of the two tasks, but counter to direct mixing, we use the compounded-label embedding described in Sec. 3 for optimization and downsample the input examples to reduce training time.

Reduced Pipeline: This is the same pipeline setup as described above, except that we reduce the model sizes for both sentence selection and verification such that the total model size is equal to all other setups that use only a single joint model. This experiment gives a fair comparison between each of the setups by canceling out the parameter-size variance. Table 1 shows a comparison of the first four different setups.

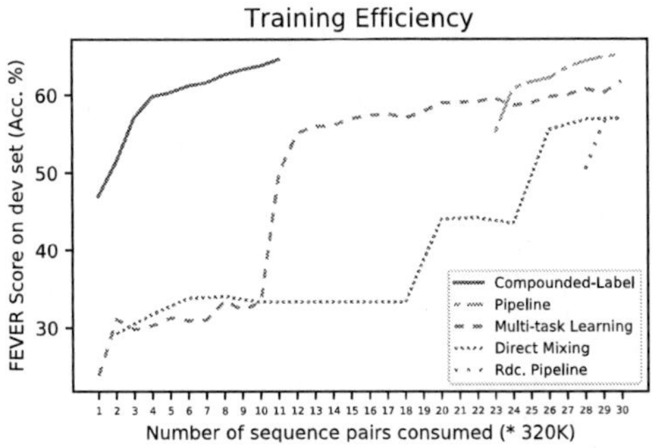

Figure 2: Model performance for different setups with respect to number of sequence pairs consumed. We only show performance until the consumption of the first 30×320K data points.

5 Results and Analysis

FEVER Score Performance: We observe from Table 2 that compounded-label training outperforms[2] both the multitask learning and direct mixing setups. We speculate that the performance gap is due to the fact that in the multi-task and direct mixing training setups, the same model is trained by separated and different supervisions of two tasks, resulting in oscillation and making it difficult to reach a better global minimum. However, in the compounded-label setup, training the model on one task always gives a subtly-controlled supervision on the other task. This not only applies natural regularization on the targeted task itself, but also pushes the model towards a better state for both tasks.

Next, we also show that the compounded-label setup achieves a higher FEVER score than the reduced-pipeline setup (3rd row in Table 2), indicating its ability to model the two tasks jointly in a more compact and parameter-efficient way. Although the full pipeline setup gives a slightly higher FEVER score, the compounded-label setup has the advantage of reducing parameter size by one-third, requiring less than half the training computation, and improving the training efficiency (elaborated on in the following subsection). Finally, we also compare recall scores, since this is most related to the FEVER score, as validated by Nie et al. (2019a).

Efficiency: In Fig. 2, we show the training efficiency of different approaches by tracking performance with the number of data points consumed.[3] Parameter update settings are equal across all experiments and thus show an accurate depiction of the speedup independent of batch size, etc. For fair comparison, there is no FEVER score for the first 22 × 320K data points in the pipeline setup since these data points are consumed in the separate upstream sentence selection training. The compounded-label training setup exhibits a more stable training curve than the other setups during initial training, and reaches a 60%+ FEVER score after seeing only 1,280K data points. This indicates that the compounded-label setting allows the model to quickly reach a stable and functional state. This is valuable for online learning on streaming data, where the model is trained with real-time human feedback. On the contrary, the performance of the multi-task learning and direct mixing setups fluctuates at a low level during initial training stages, which shows that optimization oscillation makes training difficult in these setups.

Model	FEVER	LA	F1
Pipeline	**62.69**	66.20	53.71
Compounded-Label	61.65	**66.21**	50.28

Table 3: Performance of systems on blind test results.

Blind Test Results: In Table 3 we compare the two setups on the blind test set. Compounded Label achieved 61.65% FEVER score and 66.21% label score (LA) while the pipeline setup got 62.69% and 66.20% for FEVER score and LA, respectively. Since the upper bound is dependent on document retrieval quality, we report the upper bound of these scores as 92.42% following Nie et al. (2019a). Our method was able to yield results comparable to the pipeline model on FEVER score and even higher results on label score, with simpler design, faster convergence and only two-thirds the number of parameters.

6 Conclusion

We present a simple compounded-label setup for jointly training sentence selection and claim verification. This setup provides higher training efficiency and lower parameter size while still achieving comparable results to the pipeline approach.

[2]In Table 2, the improvements of compounded-label over the first three entries are significant with $p < 10^{-5}$ while the improvement of full pipeline over compounded-label is significant with $p < 0.05$. Stat. significance was computed on bootstrap test with 100K iterations (Noreen, 1989; Efron and Tibshirani, 1994).

[3]We measure the training efficiency based on the size of data consumed until convergence rather than training time or the full training size because it gives a fair measurement about how fast the model can reach a fully-functional state independent of computational resources and platforms.

Acknowledgments

We thank the reviewers for their helpful comments. This work was supported by DARPA MCS Grant N66001-19-2-4031, and awards from Google and Facebook. The views, opinions, and/or findings contained in this article are those of the authors and should not be interpreted as representing the official views or policies, either expressed or implied, of the funding agency.

References

Isabelle Augenstein, Christina Lioma, Dongsheng Wang, Lucas Chaves Lima, Casper Hansen, Christian Hansen, and Jakob Grue Simonsen. 2019. Multifc: A real-world multi-domain dataset for evidence-based fact checking of claims. In *EMNLP*.

Isabelle Augenstein, Sebastian Ruder, and Anders Søgaard. 2018. Multi-task learning of pairwise sequence classification tasks over disparate label spaces. In *NAACL-HLT*.

Hannah Bast, Björn Buchhold, and Elmar Haussmann. 2017. Overview of the triple scoring task at the wsdm cup 2017. *WSDM Cup*.

Samuel Bowman, Gabor Angeli, Christopher Potts, and Christopher D Manning. 2015. A large annotated corpus for learning natural language inference. In *EMNLP*.

Rich Caruana. 1997. Multitask learning. *Machine learning*, 28(1):41–75.

Mostafa Dehghani, Hamed Zamani, Aliaksei Severyn, Jaap Kamps, and W Bruce Croft. 2017. Neural ranking models with weak supervision. In *SIGIR*.

Daxiang Dong, Hua Wu, Wei He, Dianhai Yu, and Haifeng Wang. 2015. Multi-task learning for multiple language translation. In *ACL*.

Bradley Efron and Robert J Tibshirani. 1994. *An introduction to the bootstrap*. CRC press.

Jiafeng Guo, Yixing Fan, Qingyao Ai, and W Bruce Croft. 2016. A deep relevance matching model for ad-hoc retrieval. In *CIKM*.

Andreas Hanselowski, Avinesh P.V.S., Benjamin Schiller, Felix Caspelherr, Debanjan * Chaudhuri, Christian M. Meyer, and Iryna Gurevych. 2018a. A retrospective analysis of the fake news challenge stance-detection task. In *COLING*.

Andreas Hanselowski, Hao Zhang, Zile Li, Daniil Sorokin, Benjamin Schiller, Claudia Schulz, and Iryna Gurevych. 2018b. Multi-sentence textual entailment for claim verification. In *Proceedings of the First Workshop on Fact Extraction and VERification (FEVER)*.

Kazuma Hashimoto, Yoshimasa Tsuruoka, Richard Socher, et al. 2017. A joint many-task model: Growing a neural network for multiple nlp tasks. In *EMNLP*.

Po-Sen Huang, Xiaodong He, Jianfeng Gao, Li Deng, Alex Acero, and Larry Heck. 2013. Learning deep structured semantic models for web search using clickthrough data. In *CIKM*.

Pengfei Liu, Xipeng Qiu, and Xuanjing Huang. 2017. Adversarial multi-task learning for text classification. *ACL*.

Minh-Thang Luong, Quoc V Le, Ilya Sutskever, Oriol Vinyals, and Lukasz Kaiser. 2016. Multi-task sequence to sequence learning. *ICLR*.

Bhaskar Mitra, Fernando Diaz, and Nick Craswell. 2017. Learning to match using local and distributed representations of text for web search. In *WWW*.

Yixin Nie, Haonan Chen, and Mohit Bansal. 2019a. Combining fact extraction and verification with neural semantic matching networks. *AAAI*.

Yixin Nie, Songhe Wang, and Mohit Bansal. 2019b. Revealing the importance of semantic retrieval for machine reading at scale. In *2019 Conference on Empirical Methods in Natural Language Processing and 9th International Joint Conference on Natural Language Processing (EMNLP-IJCNLP)*.

Eric W Noreen. 1989. *Computer-intensive methods for testing hypotheses*. Wiley New York.

Verónica Pérez-Rosas, Bennett Kleinberg, Alexandra Lefevre, and Rada Mihalcea. 2018. Automatic detection of fake news. In *COLING*.

Pomerleau and Rao. 2017. Fake news challenge.

Peng Qi, Xiaowen Lin, Leo Mehr, Zijian Wang, and Christopher D Manning. 2019. Answering complex open-domain questions through iterative query generation. *EMNLP*.

Kai Shu, Limeng Cui, Suhang Wang, Dongwon Lee, and Huan Liu. 2019a. defend: Explainable fake news detection.

Kai Shu, Suhang Wang, and Huan Liu. 2019b. Beyond news contents: The role of social context for fake news detection. ACM.

Anders Søgaard and Yoav Goldberg. 2016. Deep multi-task learning with low level tasks supervised at lower layers. In *ACL*.

James Thorne, Andreas Vlachos, Christos Christodoulopoulos, and Arpit Mittal. 2018a. FEVER: a large-scale dataset for fact extraction and verification. In *NAACL-HLT*.

James Thorne, Andreas Vlachos, Oana Cocarascu, Christos Christodoulopoulos, and Arpit Mittal. 2018b. The fact extraction and verification (fever) shared task. *arXiv preprint arXiv:1811.10971*.

Andreas Vlachos and Sebastian Riedel. 2014. Fact checking: Task definition and dataset construction. In *ACL LACSS Workshop*.

William Yang Wang. 2017. "liar, liar pants on fire": A new benchmark dataset for fake news detection. In *ACL*.

Adina Williams, Nikita Nangia, and Samuel Bowman. 2018. A broad-coverage challenge corpus for sentence understanding through inference. In *NAACL-HLT*.

Wenpeng Yin and Dan Roth. 2018. Twowingos: A two-wing optimization strategy for evidential claim verification. In *EMNLP*.

Takuma Yoneda, Jeff Mitchell, Johannes Welbl, Pontus Stenetorp, and Sebastian Riedel. 2018. Ucl machine reading group: Four factor framework for fact finding (hexaf). In *Proceedings of the First Workshop on Fact Extraction and VERification (FEVER)*.

Shuai Zhao, Bo Cheng, Hao Yang, et al. 2018. An end-to-end multi-task learning model for fact checking. In *Proceedings of the First Workshop on Fact Extraction and VERification (FEVER)*.

Jie Zhou, Xu Han, Cheng Yang, Zhiyuan Liu, Lifeng Wang, Changcheng Li, and Maosong Sun. 2019. Gear: Graph-based evidence aggregating and reasoning for fact verification. *ACL*.

A Appendix

A.1 NSMN Output Layer Modifications

The dimension of final NSMN output vector can be customized depending on the downstream task. In the pipeline setting, multi-task learning setting, and direct mixing setting, $\mathbf{m} = \langle m^+, m^- \rangle$ for sentence selection, where $m^+ \in \mathbb{R}$ is a scalar value indicating the score for selecting the current sentence as evidence and m^- gives the score for discarding it. For claim verification, $\mathbf{m} = \langle m_s, m_r, m_n \rangle$, where the elements of the vector denote the score for predicting the three labels, namely SUPPORTS, REFUTES, and NEI, respectively. However, in the compounded-label setting, $\mathbf{m} \in \mathbb{R}^4$ and the model is optimized with a compact label embedding described in the paper.

A.2 Training Details

This section includes the training details for sentence selection and verification. We use the pageview method in Nie et al. (2019a) to obtain the same upstream document retrieval data for all of our four setups.

Pipeline: In the pipeline and the reduced-size-pipeline setup, we use exactly the same training setup as in Nie et al. (2019a) for sentence selection and claim verification.

Multi-task Learning: In this setup, we choose batch as 64 and use Adam optimizer with default initial parameters. The mixing ratio for sentence selection and claim verification is set to 1 thus the two tasks are both trained alternately every two batches. As in Nie et al. (2019a), we downsample the training data for the sentence selection task at the beginning of each epoch.

Data Mixing: We use a batch size of 64 and Adam optimizer with default settings. As our two subtasks contain different amounts of training data, we use the data size ratio as the task mixing ratio within each batch. We guarantee that each label is present at least once in each mini-batch.

Compounded-Label: We use a batch size of 32 and Adam optimizer with default settings. We downsample the negative examples for sentence selection with the probability of p (this is done at the beginning of every epoch) and randomly mix and shuffle the training data for both sentence selection and claim verification into one input set and train the single model with compounded-label as described in the paper. p is set to be 0.1 at the first epoch and 0.025 otherwise. λ_1 and λ_2 are set to be 1 and 0.5 respectively.

Hyper-parameter Selection: In the experiments for multi-task learning, data mixing and compounded-label settings, the batch size is chosen from either 64 or 32 by optimizing final FEVER Score.[4] In multi-task learning, the mixing ratio of sentence selection to claim verification is tuned from $\{1, 2\}$. For the compounded-label setting, λ_1 and λ_2 are tuned from $\{1, 0.9\}$ and $\{0.45, 0.5\}$ respectively based on the intuition that supporting and refuting sentences can be also treated as positive evidence examples with high confidence while partially relevant sentences that cannot verify the claim can be treated as weakly related evidence.

[4]We observed a failure of convergence when we choose batch size as 32 in multi-task learning settings.

Stance Prediction and Claim Verification: An Arabic Perspective

Jude Khouja
Latynt
jude@latynt.com

Abstract

This work explores the application of textual entailment in news claim verification and stance prediction using a new corpus in Arabic. The publicly available corpus comes in two perspectives: a version consisting of 4,547 true and false claims and a version consisting of 3,786 pairs (claim, evidence). We describe the methodology for creating the corpus and the annotation process. Using the introduced corpus, we also develop two machine learning baselines for two proposed tasks: claim verification and stance prediction. Our best model utilizes pretraining (BERT) and achieves 76.7 *F1* on the stance prediction task and 64.3 *F1* on the claim verification task. Our preliminary experiments shed some light on the limits of automatic claim verification that relies on claims text only. Results hint that while the linguistic features and world knowledge learned during pretraining are useful for stance prediction, such learned representations from pretraining are insufficient for verifying claims without access to context or evidence.

1 Introduction

Although fake news is not an emerging phenomenon and has been documented throughout history, the prevalence and wide spread of misinformation over the internet has captured significant proportion of public attention in recent years. This is in part linked to the low barrier for content generation through the advent of the internet and social media (Allcott and Gentzkow, 2017) and the fact that false news spread faster than true news (Vosoughi et al., 2018) rendering it increasingly dangerous to public discourse. The widespread exposure in the U.S. for example has been reported by researchers who found that the average American encountered between one and three stories from known publishers of fake news during the month before the 2016 election (Allcott and Gentzkow, 2017).

Since manual fact-checking by human experts does not scale well with the amount of information shared on the web, there is a growing body of work in recent years aimed at developing automatic tools to target fake news, misinformation and credibility of content on social media in general (Rubin et al., 2016; El Ballouli et al., 2017; Baly et al., 2018a,b; Wang et al., 2018; Saleh et al., 2019; Zhang et al., 2019). Several datasets were developed to further aid research on this topic[1] (Darwish et al., 2017; Wang, 2017; Baly et al., 2018b; Thorne et al., 2018). We refer readers to (Thorne and Vlachos, 2018; Pierri and Ceri, 2019) for a more comprehensive overview of recent research on fake news, propaganda and misinformation.

Despite the increased attention, most of the work has been focusing on the English language. Tools, resources and datasets available in Arabic are limited (Darwish et al., 2017; Baly et al., 2018b; Elsayed et al., 2019). As such, this work contributes to recent efforts targeting Arabic by introducing a new publicly available corpus in Arabic that is suitable to study claim verification and semantic entailment (Katz, 1972).

2 Related Work

In recent years, there has been rapid progress in developing systems and tools for automatic fact checking and claim verification. Various approaches were developed which relied on a diverse set of methods and information to verify claims. Most relevant to this work are approaches that used content such as textual information in the title and/or body of the claims to predict their veracity. Among this direction of research those that considered a machine learning approach (Potthast et al.,

[1]FNC: http://www.fakenewschallenge.org/

Proceedings of the Third Workshop on Fact Extraction and VERification (FEVER), pages 8–17
July 9, 2020.

Given a news title, write two news titles that:
A- Paraphrase the original title: Has same meaning but is worded differently by rephrasing and changing Syntax, using verb synonyms, using different words to describe the same information such as locations, counts and dates.
B- Contradict the original title: Looks similar to the original title but has contradicting meaning (both cannot be true in the same context) by reversing meaning without negating main verb, using antonym of main verb with rephrasing, changing key information using world knowledge such as locations, counts and dates.

Table 1: Guidelines for rewriting news titles.

2017; Wang et al., 2018; Alzanin and Azmi, 2019) including deep learning techniques (Hanselowski et al., 2017; Baly et al., 2018b; Popat et al., 2018; Chawla et al., 2019; Helwe et al., 2019; Lv et al., 2019).

Datasets: There are limited but growing datasets related to claim verification (Al Zaatari et al., 2016; Darwish et al., 2017; Wang, 2017; Baly et al., 2018b; Thorne et al., 2018; Alkhair et al., 2019; Alzanin and Azmi, 2019; Elsayed et al., 2019). However, datasets focusing on Arabic remain scarce (Darwish et al., 2017; Baly et al., 2018b; Elsayed et al., 2019). Recently, work on the application of textual entailment for claim verfication has been explored and new datasets combining stance prediction and claim verfication were introduced (Baly et al., 2018b; Thorne et al., 2018).

This work is most in line with that direction. We developed a new corpus in Arabic that can be used jointly for claim verification and textual entailment recognition. However, our new corpus differs from the aforementioned datasets in that it is at the sentence level, hence, we are disentangling the tasks of claim verification and textual entailment from the task of evidence extraction (Information Retrieval) and focusing on the former. We also start from real news titles and generate true/false claims from them. Our aim is to mitigate one type of bias that results from starting with fake news collected in the wild: bias in the distribution of topics among the true/false claims. While some forms of biases about the world are useful in determining the veracity of a claim, some can be problematic. We can imagine a dataset that contains more positive[2] news in the "fake" class than in the "true" class. A system trained on such data could predict the class "fake" with higher confidence for any claim that has a positive tone compared to one that has a negative or neutral tone. Such surface level biases in topics and linguistic styles could arguably result in models that do not generalize well.

3 The corpus

In this part, we describe our Arabic News Stance (ANS) corpus.[3] We derived two perspectives of the corpus suitable for claim verification and stance classification. Please refer to Appendix A to read our data statement about the corpus.

3.1 Data Collection

In contrast to Baly et al. (2018b) and more in line with Thorne et al. (2018), we start with true news titles (reference) and generate fake/true claims from them. The corpus generating process can be summarized in two stages: 1) generating true/false modifications of existing news titles through crowdsourcing; and 2) validating the generated claims by annotating them in a separate phase.

We derive our corpus by sampling a subset of news titles from the most recent version of the Arabic News Texts (ANT) corpus (Chouigui et al., 2017); A collection of Arabic news from multiple news media sources in the Middle East. The dataset was suitable for our task as it covers several topics of news (politics, sports, *etc.*) sourced from several credible mainstream news outlets (BBC, CNN, Al Arabiya, *etc.*). The following is an example of a news title from this dataset:

حقائق سقوط صخرة تزن ١٠٠ كغ من الحائط
الغربي بالقدس

"Facts about the falling of a boulder weighing 100 kg. of the west wall in Jerusalem."

Generating true/false claims We used crowdsourcing to generate true/false claims. Starting from a news title, we recruited annotators to modify each news title into a new claim. For true claims, annotators were asked to paraphrase the original sentence by changing its syntax and wording while maintaining the integrity of the information. We allowed for the use of world knowledge to modify the information. For example, replacing cities with

[2]Positive here refers to sentiment

[3]Data available at: https://github.com/latynt/ans

Type	Translation	Arabic
Reference	**Wall Street records largest losses in 6 weeks**	وول ستريت تسجل أكبر خسائر في ٦ أسابيع
Paraphrase	Losses in Wall Street are the highest in 6 weeks	خسائر في وول ستريت هي الأعلى في ستة اسابيع
Contradiction	Profits in Wall Street in the last six weeks	مكاسب في وول ستريت في الاسابيع الستة الاخيرة
Reference	**Death of a journalist who reported on Russian Mercenaries in Syria in mysterious circumstances**	وفاة صحفي كتب عن المرتزقة الروس في سوريا في ظروف غامضة
Paraphrase	Death of a journalist in mysterious circumstances after he reported on Russian Mercenaries in Syria	وفاة صحفى فى ظروف غامضة بعد أن كتب عن المرتزقة الروس فى سوريا
Contradiction	Death of a journalist after battling with illness	وفاة صحفى بعد صراع مع المرض
Reference	**5.5 Billion withdrawn from emerging markets by investors in one week**	٥.٥ مليار دولار سحوبات المستثمرين من الأسواق الناشئة بأسبوع
Paraphrase	Nearly 6 Billion withdrawn in a week from emerging markets	قرابة ستة مليار دولار سحوبات أسبوع في الأسواق الناشئة
Contradiction	Almost a million in withdrawals from emerging markets	سحوبات حوالي المليون في الأسواق الناشئة

Table 2: Examples of modifications by annotators. Green highlights a change in line with reference. Red highlights a conflicting part of the sentence with the reference sentence.

countries and celebrities and politicians with their nationalities.

For false claims, to insure that the modification results in meaningful mutation of the semantic information, the instructions (Table 1) stated that the modified sentence should contradict the original title in such a way that both cannot simultaneously be true in the same context. Annotators were asked to avoid simple negation and were encouraged to use different strategies for modifying the sentences. Our analysis of a sample of the collected data showed that different annotators utilized different strategies at different rates. For example, some annotators predominantly altered years, counts and locations that appeared in the original titles while others modified the semantics of the modified sentences to have opposite meaning (detained vs. released, supported vs. opposed, etc.).

We relied on Amazon Mechanical Turk[4] and Upwork [5] to recruit annotators. We only considered Arabic native speakers for news title rewriting. All annotators had to pass a language qualification test similar to our task. Data was randomly assigned to annotators in batches of 500. To insure the quality of the generated data, we sampled data during the annotation from each batch and re-annotated any batch containing errors in more than 10% of the sample by resending the batch to the annotator after explaining the errors. See Table 2 for examples of generated claims using different modification strategies.

3.2 Data Validation And Analysis

To evaluate the quality of our data, we performed a second round of annotation on the generated news titles. We derived a new task in which annotators were presented with a pair of sentences and asked to supply a hypothesis about how they are semantically related. This task is related to the the semantic concepts of entailment and contradiction (Katz, 1972; Bowman et al., 2015) but with the aim of validating our generated ture/fake claims. We highlight a notable difference compared to other work on stance classification. In contrast to the commonly used four classes adopted in other datasets [6] *(agree, contradict, discuss, unrelated)*, we elect to merge labels *(discuss, unrelated)* into one *(other/not enough information)* resulting in three classes – *paraphrase, contradiction, other/not enough information* for each pair of news titles. Our motivation is that despite the general value of discriminating between irrelevant documents[7] (unrelated) and documents that are related to the claim but do not make a stance about the claim (discuss), both classes represent the same position in the context of stance prediction. We, therefore, treat them as one class. We found that this is also similar to the approach by Thorne et al. (2018).

To present annotators with a small set of the third class (other), we first considered randomly pairing news titles from our corpus. We hypothesized that randomly paired news titles will be discussing unrelated news and would naturally be assigned the label *other* by annotators. However and upon examining examples of this method, we noticed that telling the (other) class apart from the two classes was dis-proportionally trivial since the randomly paired sentences differed significantly

[4]https://www.mturk.com

[5]https://www.upwork.com/

[6]For example: Fake News Challenge (FNC)

[7]Documents in this case refer to sentences but could be any body of text. Hence, in this work we use both terms interchangeably.

Number of Annotators	#	%
3	2594	60.9%
4	1239	29.1%
5	426	10.0%
Annotator Labels Overlap	**#**	**%**
$< 75\%$	470	11.0%
75 - 99%	210	4.9%
100%	3579	84.0%
Majority/Author Labels Overlap	**#**	**%**
Majority Label = Author's Label	3766	99.4%
Majority Label $\neq$ Author's Label	23	0.6%
Fleiss k		
3 total annotators		0.83
4 total annotators		0.81
5 total annotators		0.83

Table 3: Statistics for the annotation results. The author's label is the label obtained from the worker who rewrote the news title. Majority label is the consensus of 75% or higher of the annotators.

(discussed different topics and contained no overlapping words) compared to pairs from the *paraphrase, contradict* classes. Predicting this class, therefore, can be reduced to checking for the absence of overlap in words from the paired titles. As an alternative selection criteria to random pairing, we used a similarity metric to select pairs that look more similar. We calculate the F1 score of overlapping ngrams in the paired titles weighted by the ngram size similar to Trinh and Le (2018). In our case however, we consider ngrams at the character level given the short length of the sentences. We included ngrams of size 2 to 6 and set the minimum score to 0.1.

A total of 4,259 pairs were labeled by 3 to 5 annotators. We considered the author's rewritten sentences as labels (for the *paraphrase* and *contradict* classes). Table 3 shows the annotation statistics. The Fleiss k scores (calculated separately for examples labeled by 3, 4 and 5 annotators) show overall a very high level of agreement (> 0.81) suggesting that the quality of the dataset is sufficiently high. For the final data, we included only pairs with inter annotator agreement of 75% or higher, hence, dismissing all data with 2 out of 3 majority vote or worse.

Figures 1 and 2 provide some details about the length of the written claims in the final dataset compared to the original reference sentences. We noticed that on average, claims are shorter than the original references with contradicting claims being shorter than paraphrasing claims. This could be due to workers aiming to minimize time spent per each example. Another likely explanation is the fact that contradicting a statements by replacing or removing key words is easier than paraphrasing a statement.

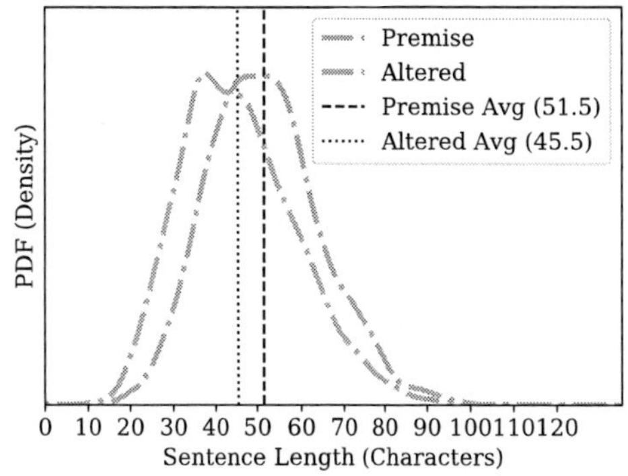

Figure 1: Length of sentences in dataset (rewritten vs. reference)

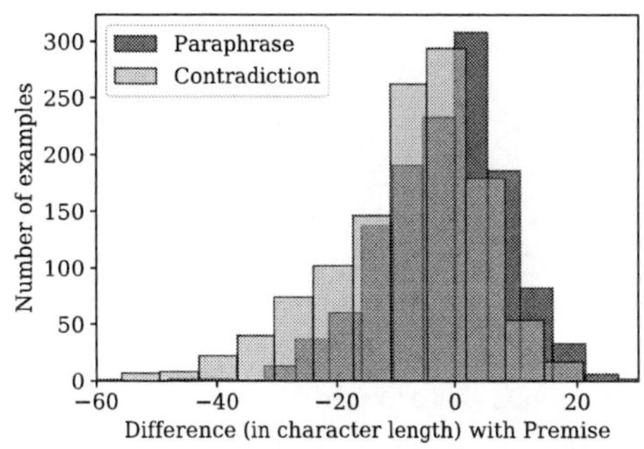

Figure 2: Comparison in rewritten sentences

4 Experiments

In this section, to demonstrate the utility of the corpus, we derive two tasks useful for evaluating news veracity and stance prediction and develop two baselines to evaluate on the proposed tasks. We describe the proposed tasks and details of the baselines in this section and the results in section 5.

4.1 Tasks

Claim Only Verification: In this setting, we explore the task of verifying claims based only on information in the claims themselves. In our corpus, we assess the veracity of a claim c_i from our corpus D based solely on the textual information of the claim. The task is, hence, a binary classification where an estimator needs to map an input to a label Y which can be either *fake* or *not fake*:

Class	#	%
Not Fake	3072	67.6%
Fake	1475	32.4%

Table 4: Class distribution for claim verification. (#: total number of examples. %: percentage of all data)

Class	#	%
Disagree	2399	63.4%
Agree	1301	34.4%
Other	86	2.3%

Table 5: Class distribution for stance prediction. (#: total number of examples. %: percentage of all data)

$$p(Y|c_i), \qquad c_i \in D$$

We consider all original news titles (reference sentences) in our corpus to belong to the *not fake* class. We rely on the fact that the reference sentences originated from reputable mainstream media in the Middle East. Our *fake* class examples consist of the sentences corrupted by annotators that passed the data validation process described in Section 3.1. Table 4 shows the distribution of classes for this task.

It is important to discern the limited scope in defining news veracity in this work: the incorrectness of the corrupted sentence is not a universal statement about the claim. We note the fact that several of the corrupted sentences can be factual/not fake in other contexts. As such, we consider them fake in regards to the related event/context - in this case our reference sentence (original news titles). Further analysis exposed two instances where the modified sentences matched other original news titles. Both examples were excluded from the corpus for this task. However, such cases hint at the limits of claim verification using claim text only. We further explore this in section 5 and share some insights.

Stance Prediction This task is a direct reflection of our annotation process. Given a reference sentence r_i and a claim c_i, predict the label Y (Agree, Contradict, Other/Not enough information) from the claim/reference pair (c_i, r_i).

$$p(Y|c_i, r_i), \qquad (c_i, r_i) \in D$$

Table 5 shows the distribution of classes in our corpus for the stance prediction task.

4.2 Methods

We evaluate two baselines on both tasks. For modeling, we considered two classes of models that have been largely adopted by the NLP community. The models are described in the next section.

Recurrent Perspective Matching: Our first baseline is a simple RNN model that uses Long Short Term Memory (LSTM) (Hochreiter and Schmidhuber, 1997) as the main building block to encode the input. LSTM models encode the input sequentially and can model temporal dependencies useful to semantic tasks. In our implementation for both tasks, we consider both character level and word level representations of the input sentence(s) separately. In each case, we represent every input word/character with a unique d-dimensional vector that is learned during training. These vectors are then passed through the LSTM layer in sequence and the output of the last step (at the end of the sentence) is used as the encoding of the sentence(s). For the claim verification task, the claim encoding $\overrightarrow{h}_t$ can be described by:

$$\overrightarrow{h}_t = \overrightarrow{LSTM}(\overrightarrow{h}_{t-1}, x_t) \qquad t = 1, ..., M_i$$

Where M_i is the length size of the sentence corresponding to example i and x_t is the character/word at position t.
In stance prediction, the input consists of a pair of sentences (reference r, claim c). Each is encoded using the same LSTM layer to obtain their encoding:

$$\overrightarrow{r}_t = \overrightarrow{LSTM}(\overrightarrow{r}_{t-1}, x_t) \qquad t = 1, ..., M_i^r$$
$$\overrightarrow{c}_t = \overrightarrow{LSTM}(\overrightarrow{c}_{t-1}, x_t) \qquad t = 1, ..., M_i^k$$

To obtain the interaction representation $\overrightarrow{h}_t$, $\overrightarrow{\mathrm{r}_t}$ and $\overrightarrow{\mathrm{c}_t}$ are multiplied element-wise. We experimented with *cosine* similarity and concatenation and found the element-wise multiplication and concatenation to work slightly better than *cosine* similarity:

$$\overrightarrow{h}_t = (\overrightarrow{\mathrm{r}_t} \circ \overrightarrow{k}_t)$$

The resulting encoding in both tasks $\overrightarrow{h}_t$ is then passed through a linear layer with non-linearity

		(dev)				(test)		
Claim Verification	**Acc.**	**Prec.**	**Rec.**	F_1	**Acc.**	**Prec.**	**Rec.**	F_1
Majority Class	68.1	34.1	50.0	40.5	67.1	33.6	50.0	40.2
LSTM character level								
char, 10(emb), 100(hid), 0(dropout)	70.2	65.7	56.8	55.4	67.3	60.2	54.6	52.5
char, 10(emb), 100(hid), 30.0(dropout)	70.6	67.9	56.5	54.6	67.8	61.3	55.1	53.1
LSTM word level								
word, 50(emb), 50(hid), 0(dropout)	68.1	60.4	54.8	52.9	65.8	57.2	53.9	52.4
word, 50(emb), 100(hid), 0(dropout)	68.6	61.8	56.4	55.5	64.5	55.4	53.3	52.1
Stance Prediction								
Majority Class	62.4	20.8	33.3	25.6	63.8	21.3	33.3	26.0
LSTM character level								
char, 10(emb), 50(hid), 0(dropout)	62.2	20.7	33.3	25.6	64.4	21.5	33.3	26.1
char, 50(emb), 50(hid), 0(dropout)	62.4	20.8	33.3	25.6	64.1	21.4	33.3	26.0
char, 50(emb), 50(hid), 30.0(dropout)	62.5	43.0	33.7	26.6	64.4	46.4	34.0	27.5
LSTM word level								
word, 10(emb), 50(hid), 0(dropout)	62.1	38.7	39.2	38.8	62.0	37.8	38.1	37.8
word, 50(emb), 50(hid), 30.0(dropout)	63.0	39.9	40.7	40.3	59.8	37.4	38.2	37.8

Table 6: Results for the claim verification and stance prediction Tasks.

(*ReLu*) followed by a $softmax$ function to convert the output to probabilities for each class:

$$p(Y = c|h_i) = softmax(ReLu(W_c\overrightarrow{h_i} + b_c))$$

W_c and b_c are learnable parameters associated with each class c in the corresponding task.
Prediction in both tasks is done by selecting the label with the highest probability:

$$\arg\max_c p(Y = c|h_i)$$

Pretrained Transformer: Pretraining and transfer learning (Devlin et al., 2018a; Peters et al., 2018; Radford et al., 2019) has recently gained attention as a popular approach to acquiring universal linguistic features useful in many downstream NLP tasks and was shown to be successful in improving on the state of the art in many downstream NLP tasks with minimal fine-tuning. Lv et al. (2019) have successfully explored BERT for the task of fake news detection in English and proposed an extension that improves on fine-tuned BERT. In addition to the aforementioned supervised methods, we evaluate BERT (Devlin et al., 2018a) on both tasks in our corpus. We are not aware of any other work that explored pretraining for claim verification and stance prediction in Arabic.

BERT is based on the Transformer model first introduced by Vaswani et al. (2017). Transformer-based models have recently become common in many NLP tasks including question answering and entailment classification (Devlin et al., 2018b; Radford, 2018). For both tasks, we utilize a publicly available implementation that has been trained on a multilingual dataset including Arabic.[8]. We elect to adhere to the proposed approach recommended by Devlin et al. (2018a) for future reproducibility. Since our implementation is identical to the one provided by the authors, we will omit the detailed description of the model architecture and refer readers to (Vaswani et al., 2017)[9].

Task	**Prec.**	**Rec.**	F_1
Claim Verification			
Fake	51	55	53
Not Fake	77	75	76
Macro Avg.	**64.1**	**64.6**	**64.3**
Stance Detection			
Agree	65	63	64
Disagree	80	81	80
Other	86	86	86
Macro Avg.	**76.8**	**76.6**	**76.7**

Table 7: Results of using pretraining (BERT) on claim verification and stance prediction tasks.

5 Results

For the recurrent perspective models, we trained all models for 100 epochs using Adam optimizer (Kingma and Ba, 2014) with 0.001 learning rate. We conducted hyper-parameter tuning on the de-

[8]We use BERT-Base, Multilingual Cased: 104 languages, 12-layer, 768-hidden, 12-heads, 110M parameters

[9]See also: http://nlp.seas.harvard.edu/2018/04/03/attention.html

Prediction	Label	Translation	Arabic
Fake	Fake	Historic agreement between Europe and Japan to support trump	اتفاق تاريخي بين أوروبا و اليابان لمساعدة ترامب
Fake	True	Historic agreement between Europe and Japan to confront trump	اتفاق تاريخي بين أوروبا و اليابان لمواجهة ترامب
True	Fake	First women's interest channel in Gaza soon to see the light	أول قناة تلفزيونية نسائية في غزة تظهر للنور قريبا
True	True	First women's interest channel in Gaza faces uncertain fate	أول قناة تلفزيونية نسائية في غزة تواجه مصيرا مجهولا
Fake	True	Ethiopia assures Egypt of its Nile share	أثيوبيا تؤكد حرصها على حصة مصر بالنيل
Fake	Fake	Ethiopia apathetic about Egypt's right of the Nile water	أثيوبيا غير معنية بحصة مصر من مياه النيل

Table 8: Examples of claim verification task predictions using fine-tuned BERT highlighting the model's invariant labels for similar sentences with different meanings.

velopment set. For the pretrained BERT model, we fine-tune on our data for 3 epochs using BERT BPE units.

Table 6 shows the top results of all experiments for both tasks. We report the accuracy and F_1 (Macro unweighted average). In the claim verification task, results show that in general, word based models perform comparably to character based models but we note that all results do not provide significant gains (53.1 vs. 40.2 F_1) compared to the baseline (majority class) which could be explained by the small training data size but might hint at an ill-defined task. We explore this further below. In the stance prediction task, experiments show word based models outperform character based models (37.8 vs 27.5 F_1). This could be due to the limited size of our corpus which is not sufficient for character based models to learn words and phrases from scratch and capture the semantic representation needed for stance prediction.

Results for the pretraining experiments (shown in Table 7) show significant improvement of the pretrained model over the models trained only on our corpus. This is similar to findings by Lv et al. (2019). However, the improvement is disproportionally larger in the stance prediction task (76.7 vs. 37.8 F_1) and the large gains do not carry over to the claim verification task (64.3 vs. 53.1 F_1). The imbalance in gains also confirms our intuition about the limitation of claim only verification which we discuss next.

Limits Of Claim Only Verification: We briefly mentioned in Section 4.1 the limited scope of claim verification in a setting were the decision about the veracity of a claim can be made using only the text of the claim. We hypothesize that the task might not be learnable through a direct mapping from the claim text to the veracity space. Given that the initial results of the fine-tuned BERT model supported this intuition, we elected to manually inspect a sample of the predictions and noticed that in many cases the model was predicting the same label for claims that look similar but are semantically different. We share a sample of these cases in Table 8. This suggests that while the linguistic features learned during pretraining were useful for textual entailment (stance prediction task), the veracity of a claim cannot be made using only implicit world knowledge learned during pretraining. A simple example highlighting this limitation is the reference news title الذهب يصعد مع تراجع الدولار *"Gold prices increase amidst a falling dollar."'* and its contradicted rewritten version "أسعار الذهب تهبط عالمياً" *"Gold prices fall globally"*. Here, it is easy to argue that the contradiction can be true in another context and hence, a decision about the veracity of this claim should only be made in reference to a particular context/event. We believe that explicitly associating each claim with evidence or context is the more appropriate approach for claim verification.

These initial experiments suggest that discriminate models trained using claim only information might rely on biases in the topics, linguistic styles, tones and implicit world-knowledge learned from training data to make predictions. Results of the performance of such models could, therefore, be inflated if the training data is not uniformly distributed across languages, topics, writing styles, political ideologies etc. While we believe that our dataset collection process which yields classes that share the same distribution of topics and news sources mitigated these types of biases, we also note that the annotation process and human factor introduced other types of biases that could be present in the data.

6 Conclusion

In this work we presented a new publicly available corpus for textual entailment and its use in studying misinformation in the Arabic language. We shared some insights about the creation of the corpus and the baselines developed to evaluate the corpus. We further explored the use of pretraining (Devlin et al., 2018a) and developed a strong baseline for our tasks. Our experiments additionally shed light on the limits of "claim-only" misinformation detection methods that rely solely on the stated claims without use of accompanying evidence. We hope to explore this further in future work. As we plan to also explore the use of generated data in studying the robustness of misinformation detection methods against adversarial data with varying linguistic styles, political ideologies and world-knowledge.

Acknowledgements

We are grateful for Ayah Zirikly, Bart Desmet and René F. Kizilcec for their valuable insights, critical commentary and helpful discussions during the course of this work. We also thank our anonymous reviewers for their thoughtful comments and suggestions.

References

Ayman Al Zaatari, Rim El Ballouli, Shady ELbassouni, Wassim El-Hajj, Hazem Hajj, Khaled Shaban, Nizar Habash, and Emad Yahya. 2016. Arabic corpora for credibility analysis. In *Proceedings of the Tenth International Conference on Language Resources and Evaluation (LREC'16)*, pages 4396–4401.

Maysoon Alkhair, Karima Meftouh, Kamel Smaïli, and Nouha Othman. 2019. An arabic corpus of fake news: Collection, analysis and classification. In *Arabic Language Processing: From Theory to Practice*, pages 292–302. Springer International Publishing.

Hunt Allcott and Matthew Gentzkow. 2017. Social media and fake news in the 2016 election. *J. Econ. Perspect.*, 31(2):211–236.

Samah M Alzanin and Aqil M Azmi. 2019. Rumor detection in arabic tweets using semi-supervised and unsupervised expectation–maximization. *Knowledge-Based Systems*, 185:104945.

Ramy Baly, Georgi Karadzhov, Dimitar Alexandrov, James Glass, and Preslav Nakov. 2018a. Predicting factuality of reporting and bias of news media sources.

Ramy Baly, Mitra Mohtarami, James Glass, Lluis Marquez, Alessandro Moschitti, and Preslav Nakov. 2018b. Integrating stance detection and fact checking in a unified corpus.

Emily Bender and Batya Friedman. 2018. Data statements for natural language processing: Toward mitigating system bias and enabling better science. *Transactions of the Association for Computational Linguistics*, 6(0):587–604.

Samuel R Bowman, Gabor Angeli, Christopher Potts, and Christopher D Manning. 2015. Learning natural language inference from a large annotated corpus. In *Proceedings of the 2015 Conference on Empirical Methods in Natural Language Processing*, pages 632–642.

Piyush Chawla, Diego Esteves, Karthik Pujar, and Jens Lehmann. 2019. SimpleLSTM: A Deep-Learning approach to Simple-Claims classification. In *Progress in Artificial Intelligence*, pages 244–255. Springer International Publishing.

A Chouigui, O B Khiroun, and B Elayeb. 2017. ANT corpus: An arabic news text collection for textual classification. In *2017 IEEE/ACS 14th International Conference on Computer Systems and Applications (AICCSA)*, pages 135–142.

Kareem Darwish, Walid Magdy, and Tahar Zanouda. 2017. Improved stance prediction in a user similarity feature space. In *Proceedings of the 2017 IEEE/ACM international conference on advances in social networks analysis and mining 2017*, pages 145–148.

Jacob Devlin, Ming-Wei Chang, Kenton Lee, and Kristina Toutanova. 2018a. BERT: Pre-training of deep bidirectional transformers for language understanding.

Jacob Devlin, Ming-Wei Chang, Kenton Lee, and Kristina Toutanova. 2018b. BERT: pre-training of deep bidirectional transformers for language understanding. *CoRR*, abs/1810.04805.

Rim El Ballouli, Wassim El-Hajj, Ahmad Ghandour, Shady Elbassuoni, Hazem Hajj, and Khaled Shaban. 2017. CAT: Credibility analysis of Arabic content on twitter. In *Proceedings of the Third Arabic Natural Language Processing Workshop*, pages 62–71, Valencia, Spain. Association for Computational Linguistics.

Tamer Elsayed, Preslav Nakov, Alberto Barrón-Cedeño, Maram Hasanain, Reem Suwaileh, Giovanni Da San Martino, and Pepa Atanasova. 2019. Overview of the CLEF-2019 CheckThat! lab: Automatic identification and verification of claims.

Andreas Hanselowski, P V S Avinesh, Benjamin Schiller, and Felix Caspelherr. 2017. Description of the system developed by team athene in the fnc-1. *Fake News Challenge*.

Chadi Helwe, Shady Elbassuoni, Ayman Al Zaatari, and Wassim El-Hajj. 2019. Assessing arabic weblog credibility via deep co-learning. In *Proceedings of the Fourth Arabic Natural Language Processing Workshop*, pages 130–136.

S Hochreiter and J Schmidhuber. 1997. Long short-term memory. *Neural Comput.*, 9(8):1735–1780.

Jerrold J Katz. 1972. *Semantic Theory*. New York: Harper & Row.

Diederik P Kingma and Jimmy Ba. 2014. Adam: A method for stochastic optimization.

Zhengwei Lv, Duoxing Liu, Haifeng Sun, Xiao Liang, Tao Lei, Zhizhong Shi, Feng Zhu, and Lei Yang. 2019. AUTOHOME-ORCA at SemEval-2019 task 8: Application of BERT for fact-checking in community forums. In *Proceedings of the 13th International Workshop on Semantic Evaluation*, pages 870–876.

Matthew E Peters, Mark Neumann, Mohit Iyyer, Matt Gardner, Christopher Clark, Kenton Lee, and Luke Zettlemoyer. 2018. Deep contextualized word representations.

Francesco Pierri and Stefano Ceri. 2019. False news on social media: A Data-Driven survey.

Kashyap Popat, Subhabrata Mukherjee, Andrew Yates, and Gerhard Weikum. 2018. DeClarE: Debunking fake news and false claims using Evidence-Aware deep learning.

Martin Potthast, Johannes Kiesel, Kevin Reinartz, Janek Bevendorff, and Benno Stein. 2017. A stylometric inquiry into hyperpartisan and fake news.

Alec Radford. 2018. Improving language understanding by generative pre-training.

Alec Radford, Jeffrey Wu, Rewon Child, David Luan, Dario Amodei, and Ilya Sutskever. 2019. Language models are unsupervised multitask learners. *OpenAI Blog*, 1(8):9.

Victoria Rubin, Niall Conroy, Yimin Chen, and Sarah Cornwell. 2016. Fake news or truth? using satirical cues to detect potentially misleading news. In *Proceedings of the Second Workshop on Computational Approaches to Deception Detection*, pages 7–17, San Diego, California. Association for Computational Linguistics.

Abdelrhman Saleh, Ramy Baly, Alberto Barrón-Cedeño, Giovanni Da San Martino, Mitra Mohtarami, Preslav Nakov, and James Glass. 2019. Team QCRI-MIT at SemEval-2019 task 4: Propaganda analysis meets hyperpartisan news detection.

James Thorne and Andreas Vlachos. 2018. Automated fact checking: Task formulations, methods and future directions.

James Thorne, Andreas Vlachos, Christos Christodoulopoulos, and Arpit Mittal. 2018. FEVER: a large-scale dataset for fact extraction and VERification.

Trieu H Trinh and Quoc V Le. 2018. A simple method for commonsense reasoning.

Ashish Vaswani, Noam Shazeer, Niki Parmar, Jakob Uszkoreit, Llion Jones, Aidan N Gomez, Lukasz Kaiser, and Illia Polosukhin. 2017. Attention is all you need. (Nips).

Soroush Vosoughi, Deb Roy, and Sinan Aral. 2018. The spread of true and false news online. *Science*, 359(6380):1146–1151.

William Yang Wang. 2017. "liar, liar pants on fire": A new benchmark dataset for fake news detection.

Yaqing Wang, Fenglong Ma, Zhiwei Jin, Ye Yuan, Guangxu Xun, Kishlay Jha, Lu Su, and Jing Gao. 2018. Eann: Event adversarial neural networks for multi-modal fake news detection. In *Proceedings of the 24th ACM SIGKDD International Conference on Knowledge Discovery Data Mining*, KDD '18, page 849–857, New York, NY, USA. Association for Computing Machinery.

Yifan Zhang, Giovanni Da San Martino, Alberto Barrón-Cedeño, Salvatore Romeo, Jisun An, Haewoon Kwak, Todor Staykovski, Israa Jaradat, Georgi Karadzhov, Ramy Baly, Kareem Darwish, James Glass, and Preslav Nakov. 2019. Tanbih: Get to know what you are reading.

A Data Statement

In line with recent efforts addressing ethical issues that can result from the use of data and technology and following the recommendations of Bender and Friedman (2018), we are sharing the following information that we believed is relevant to our dataset and the collection process. We encourage future use of the data to include a summary of this information.

A.1 Language Variety

To study and build tools in the areas of stance prediction and claim verification. Data was selected from news titles and rewritten by annotators for the purpose of generating statements and statement pairs. Part of the dataset was a random subset of the ANT corpus which was created through webcrawling news sources in the Middle East. As different tools and annotation were included in the creation of the data, we expect the distribution of topics, opinions and language to incorporate different types and levels of bias. To the best of our knowledge, the data is in Standard Arabic ('arb') with few exceptions such as abbreviations. At least Latin script ('Latn') is present.

A.2 Annotator Demographic

A total of 8 crowd-source workers mostly from the Middle East contributed to the annotations. Annotators were selected based on their fluency in the Arabic language. Demographic information was not available at the time annotation for all recruited individuals. Of the information available, we are aware of at least 1 woman, 2 men and 3 individuals who are Arabic native speakers.

A.3 Text Characteristics

The dataset includes a subset of the news titles from ANT news corpus (v2.1) which included 5 news sources (BBC, Al Arabiya, CNN, Sky News, France24) and 6 categories (culture, economy, international news, Middle East, sport, technology) collected from February 2018 to October 2018. Data also includes rewritten versions of the news titles by the annotators following the provided guidelines (see Table 1).

A Probabilistic Model with Commonsense Constraints for Pattern-based Temporal Fact Extraction

Yang Zhou[1], **Tong Zhao, Meng Jiang**
Department of Computer Science and Engineering
University of Notre Dame, Notre Dame, IN 46556
{yzhou24, tzhao2, mjiang2}@nd.edu

Abstract

Textual patterns (e.g., `Country`'s president `Person`) are specified and/or generated for extracting factual information from unstructured data. Pattern-based information extraction methods have been recognized for their efficiency and transferability. However, not every pattern is reliable: A major challenge is to derive the most complete and accurate facts from diverse and sometimes conflicting extractions. In this work, we propose a probabilistic graphical model which formulates fact extraction in a generative process. It automatically infers true facts and pattern reliability without any supervision. It has two novel designs specially for temporal facts: (1) it models pattern reliability on two types of time signals, including temporal tag in text and text generation time; (2) it models commonsense constraints as observable variables. Experimental results demonstrate that our model significantly outperforms existing methods on extracting true temporal facts from news data.

1 Introduction

Temporal fact extraction is to extract (entity, value, time)-factual tuples from text data (e.g., news, tweets) for specific attributes. It acts as one of the fundamental tasks in knowledge base construction, knowledge graph population, and question answering. For example, if we were interested in *country's president*, the entity would be of type `Location.Country`, the value would be of type `Person`, and the time would be a valid year in the person's presidential term. Thanks to name entity recognition (NER) and typing systems (Del Corro et al., 2015), pattern-based information extraction methods generate patterns consisted of entity types (Jiang et al., 2017; Li et al., 2018; Reimers et al., 2016). They are widely used for good transferability across domains and datasets, unsupervised manner requiring no or very few annotations, and high efficiency. The typed patterns give only the association between entity and value. Two types of time signals can be attached to the pairs, forming temporal triples: One is temporal tag in text, e.g., the year tag next to the entity/value mentions in the sentence; the other is text generation time, i.e., the year the text document was posted. For example, given two sentences:

1) "*... The former French [`Country`: France] president Jacques Chirac [`Person`], a self-styled affable rogue who was head of state from 1995 [temporal tag] to 2007 ...*" (posted on Sept. 26, 2019 [text generation time])

2) "*... Emmanuel Macron [`Person`], now President of France [`Country`], graduated from ENA in 2004 [temporal tag] ...*" (posted on Sept. 19, 2019 [text generation time])

Pattern-based methods discover two patterns:

- P1: former `Country` president `Person`
- P2: `Person`, now president of `Country`,

Then the methods can extract the following tuples. We label ✓ and ✗ for correct tuples and incorrect ones, respectively:

✓ (France, Jacques Chirac, 1995): P1 and temporal tag;
✗ (France, Jacques Chirac, 2019): P1 and text gen. time;
✗ (France, Emmanuel Macron, 2004): P2 and temporal tag;
✓ (France, Emmanuel Macron, 2019): P2 and text gen. time.

We have the following observations:

- **O1:** Not every pattern is reliable: the pattern "`Person` visited `Country`" is very likely to be unreliable. Not every pattern is unreliable: the pattern "current `Country`'s president `Person`" is very likely to be reliable. The above two pattern examples are somehow half and half. So, patterns have reliability.
- **O2:** For temporal fact extraction, different types of time signals might be either reliable

[1]This work was done when the first author was a visiting undergraduate student at Notre Dame.

Proceedings of the Third Workshop on Fact Extraction and VERification (FEVER), pages 18–25
July 9, 2020.

or unreliable depending on the pattern. So, there is a dependency between pattern and type of time signal, in terms of reliability.

Existing truth finding approaches assumed that a structured "source-object-claim" database was given and then estimated the reliability of source for inferring whether the claim was true or false (Yin et al., 2008; Zhao and Han, 2012; Zhao et al., 2012). For example, a source could be a book seller, an object could be a book's author list, and a claim could be an author list that a seller gave for a book. One conclusion was that *probabilistic graphical models* (PGM) (Zhao and Han, 2012; Zhao et al., 2012) have advantages of estimating source reliability over the general data distributions, compared with bootstrapping algorithms (Yin et al., 2008; Li et al., 2018; Wang et al., 2019). However, PGM-based truth finding models have not yet been developed for the task of *information extraction*. Estimating the reliability of textual patterns is new (O1). Moreover, when we focus on temporal fact extraction, modeling the dependency between pattern and type of time signals is also new (O2).

In truth finding, it is critical to define conflicts. For the book seller's example, we assume that one book can have only one true author list; so if we knew one list was true, then any different list of the same book would be false. This originated from our commonsense. Fortunately, we have quite a few commonsense rules for temporal facts, i.e., specific attributes. On *country's president*, we know that

- one president serves only one country;
- one country has only one president at a time;
- however, one country can have multiple presidents in the history (e.g., USA, France).

For the attribute *sports team's player*, we have commonsense rules:

- one player serves only one club at a time;
- however, one club has multiple players and one player can serve multiple clubs in his/her career.

We generalize possible commonsense rules:

- C1: one value matches with only one entity;
- C2: one entity matches with only one value;
- C3: one value matches with only one entity at a time;
- C4: one entity matches with only one value at a time.

So, we know that the attribute *country's president* follows C1 and C4; and the attribute *sports team's player* follows C3. The third challenge (O3) is the necessity of modeling the commonsense (e.g., C1–C4) for identifying conflicts, estimating pattern reliability, and finding true temporal facts.

To address the three challenges (O1–O3), we propose a novel Probabilistic Graphical Model with Commonsense Constraints (PGMCC), for finding true temporal facts from the results from pattern-based methods. The given input is the observed frequency of tuples extracted by a particular pattern and attached with a particular type of time signal. We model information source as a pair of pattern and type of time signal. We represent the source reliability as an unobserved variable. It becomes a generative process. We first generate a source. Next we generate a (entity, value, time)-tuple. Then we generate the frequency based on the source reliability and the tuple's trustworthiness (i.e., probability of being a truth). Moreover, we generate variables according to the commonsense rules if needed – the variable counts the values/entities that can be matched to one entity/value with or without a time constraint (at one time) from the set of *true* tuples. Given a huge number of patterns (i.e., 57,472) and tuples (i.e., 116,631) in our experiments, our proposed unsupervised learning model PGMCC can effectively estimate pattern reliability and find true temporal facts.

Our main contributions are:

- We introduce the idea of PGM-based truth finding to the task of pattern-based temporal fact extraction.
- We propose a new unsupervised probabilistic model with observed constraints to model the reliability of textual patterns, the trustworthiness of temporal tuples, and the commonsense rules for certain types of facts.
- Experimental results show that our model can improve AUC and F1 by more than 7% over the state-of-the-art.

The rest of this paper is organized as follows. Section 2 introduces the terminology and defines the problem. Section 3 presents an overview as well as details of the proposed model. Experimental results can be found in Section 4. Section 5 surveys the literature. Section 7 concludes the paper.

2 Terminology and Problem Definition

2.1 Terminology

Definition 1 (Temporal fact: (entity, value, time)-tuple)). *Let* $\mathcal{F} = \{f_1, f_2, f_3, \dots\}$ *be the set of temporal facts. Each fact* f *is in the format of* *(entity, value, time). $\mathcal{F}$ was extracted by textual pattern-based methods.*

Definition 2 (Pattern s). *Let $\mathcal{P}^{(*)} = \{p_1^{(*)}, \dots\}$ be the set of pattern source, here $* \in \{post, tag\}$ stands for the type of time signal (i.e., "text gen. time" and "temporal tag"). One pattern paired with different types of time signals will be treated as different pattern sources.*

Definition 3 (Extraction). *Let $\mathcal{E} = \{e_1, e_2, e_3, \dots\}$ be the set of extractions. Our generative model will take $\mathcal{E}$ as input. An extraction item e is in the format of $(f,\ p^{(*)},\ o)$. Here o stands for the observed frequency of fact tuples f that were extracted by pattern $p^{(*)}$ in $\mathcal{E}$.*

Definition 4 (Constraint). *Each commonsense rule (constraint) is represented as a variable. The variable is likely to be observed as 1. Examples:*

- *one `value` matches with only one `entity`, denoted as C_{1v-1e} that counts the number of such entities.*
- *one `entity` at one `time` matches with only one `value`, denoted as $C_{1(e,t)-1v}$ that counts the number of values.*

2.2 Problem Definition

Suppose the set of extractions $\mathcal{E}$ have been obtained by pattern-based methods from text data. We define the problem as follows: **Given** a set of extractions $\mathcal{E}$, pattern sources $\mathcal{P}^{(*)}$, and the constraints C_a for attribute a, **infer** truth $\mathcal{T}$ for all temporal facts $\mathcal{F}$ contained in $\mathcal{E}$ and quality information for each pattern source $p^{(*)}$.

3 Proposed Approach

We mainly discussed the model detail of PGM with multiple Constraints $C_{1(e,t)-1v}$ and C_{1v-1e}, since it's the most complicated scenario while modeling constraint. The given input is the observed frequency of fact tuples extracted by a particular pattern and attached with a particular type of time signal. Figure 1 gives the plate notation of our model. Each node represent a variable. Blue nodes indicate hyper-parameter. Gray nodes stand for observable variable. And white nodes stand for latent variables we want to infer.

3.1 Generative Process

Our approach based on PGM is a generative process. We first generate a source. Next we generate a (entity, value, time)-tuple. Then we generate the

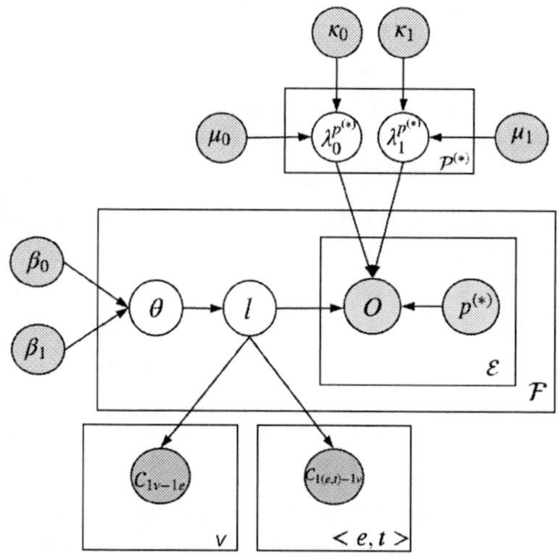

Figure 1: Probabilistic Graphic Model with Commonsense Constraint $\{C_{1(e,t)-1v}, C_{1(v)-1e}\}$

frequency based on the source reliability and the tuple's trustworthiness. Moreover, we generate variables according to the commonsense constraints. The variables counts the values/entities that can be matched to one entity/value with or without a time constraint (at one time) from the set of true tuples. The concrete meaning of each variable has been given in Table 1.

Temporal fact trustworthiness. For each temporal fact $f \in \mathcal{F}$, we first draw θ_f, i.e., the prior truth probability of fact f, from a *Beta* distribution with hyper-parameter β_0 and β_1:

$$\theta_f \sim Beta(\beta_0, \beta_1). \tag{1}$$

β_0 and β_1 represent the prior distribution of fact reliability. In practice, if we have a strong prior knowledge about how likely all or certain temporal facts are true, we can model it with the corresponding hyper-parameters. Otherwise, if we do not have a strong belief, we set a uniform prior, which means it's equally likely to be true or false, and our model can still infer the truth from other factors. After drawing the θ_f, we generate the truth label l_f from a *Bernoulli* distribution with parameter θ_f:

$$l_f \sim Bernoulli(\theta_f). \tag{2}$$

Pattern source reliability. As aforementioned, a reliable pattern source is more likely to extract true facts with higher counts, and extract false facts

Table 1: Symbols and their descriptions.

Symbol	Description
θ_f	$[0,1]$, trustworthiness of temporal fact tuple f
l_f	Boolean: label of temporal fact f
o_e	Integer: the observed frequency of fact f_e extracted by pattern $p_e^{(*)}$
$\lambda_0^{p^{(*)}}, \lambda_1^{p^{(*)}}$	Real numbers: reliability of pattern $p^{(*)}$ on giving false/true fact tuples
C_{1v-1e}	Real number: the number of entities given one value v
$C_{1(e,t)-1v}$	Real number: the sum of values given one entity e and one time t
Hyper-Parameter	
μ_0, μ_1	Integers: prior counts of false/true tuples extracted by a textual pattern
κ_0, κ_1	Integers: prior sums of false/true tuples extracted by a textual pattern
β_0, β_1	Integers: prior counts of false/true tuples

with lower counts. Therefore, we choose average count of false/true as latent pattern reliable weight, it's represented as $\lambda_0^{p^{(*)}}, \lambda_1^{p^{(*)}}$ for pattern $p^{(*)}$. The Gamma distribution is utilized because it is the conjugate prior of Poisson distributions. Initially, these two parameters are generated from *Gamma* distribution with hyper-parameter $\{\mu_0, \kappa_0\}$/$\{\mu_1, \kappa_1\}$, respectively. μ_0 and μ_1 represent the prior number of false/true fact the pattern extract, and κ_0 and κ_1 determine the prior sum of false/true fact count:

$$\lambda_0^{p^{(*)}} \sim Gamma(\mu_0, \kappa_0); \tag{3}$$

$$\lambda_1^{p^{(*)}} \sim Gamma(\mu_1, \kappa_1) \tag{4}$$

Extraction observation. For each extraction e $\in \mathcal{E}$, it is composed of $\{f, p^{(*)}, o\}$. f_e denotes the temporal fact f belongs to e, $p^{(*)}$ denotes where it's extracted, o_e stands for extraction e's observation count. When the truth label of fact f_e is false, o_e is generated from *Poisson* distribution with $p^{(*)}$'s false speaking side parameter $\lambda_0^{p^{(*)}}$. While f_e is true, o_e is generated from Poisson Distribution with $p^{(*)}$'s true speaking side parameter $\lambda_1^{p^{(*)}}$:

$$\begin{aligned} o_e &\sim Poisson(\lambda_0^{p^{(*)}}) \quad \text{if } l_{f_e} = 0, \\ o_e &\sim Poisson(\lambda_1^{p^{(*)}}) \quad \text{if } l_{f_e} = 1. \end{aligned} \tag{5}$$

Constraints. Finally, we draw the constraint variables. In temporal fact extraction, we define two variables $C_{1(e,t)-1v}$ and C_{1v-1e}. $C_{1(e,t)-1v}$ limits the number of truth on certain constraint key $\{e, t\}$. There are as many $C_{1(e,t)-1v}$ variables as unique $\{e, t\}$ keys:

$$C_{e,t} = \sum_f l_f, \quad f \in \mathcal{F}_{e,t}, \tag{6}$$

where $\mathcal{F}_{e,t}$ denotes a set of f with same $\{e, t\}$. Each $C_{1(e,t)-1v}$ is generated by $\mathcal{F}_{e,t}$ set.

C_{1v-1e} ilimits the truth of fact with same $\{v\}$:

$$C_v = \sum_{e \in E} l_{e,v} \quad \begin{cases} l_{e,v} = 1, & \text{if } \exists l_f = 1, \\ & f \in \mathcal{F}_{e,v}; \\ l_{e,v} = 0, & \text{otherwise.} \end{cases} \tag{7}$$

where $\mathcal{F}_v$ denotes set of fact with value v, $\mathcal{F}_{e,v}$ stands for a set of temporal fact f with same $\{e, v\}$, $\mathcal{F}_{e,v} \in \mathcal{F}_v$. $l_{e,v}$ denoted the truth label of v, e. Each C_{1v-1e} is generated by $\mathcal{F}_v$. If there is true fact $f \in \mathcal{F}_{e,v}$, then $l_{e,v}$ equals to one, otherwise, $l_{e,v}$ equal with zero.

4 Experiments

4.1 Dataset

We focus on attribute *country's president* and experiment on the same data set in the work of (Wang et al., 2019). It has 9,876,086 news articles (4 billion words) published from 1994–2010. We have 57,472 patterns, 116,631 temporal fact tuples, and 1,326,164 extractions. The dataset's ground truth was collected from Google and Wikipedia. It includes 3,175 true temporal facts of 130 countries.

4.2 Experiment Settings

4.2.1 Competitive methods

We compare our model with:

- TRUTHFINDER (Yin et al., 2008): It was a bootstrapping algorithm for structured data using C_{1v-1e}.
- LTM(Zhao and Han, 2012): It was a probabilistic model, assuming that the truth about an object contains more than one value. We set "object" as {entity, time} and set value as the temporal fact's value.

Table 2: Our proposed model performs better than baseline methods on finding temporal facts.

Method	**Constraints**		**Evaluation Setting**			
	e: `Country`; v: `Person`; t: year		On (e,v,t)		On $(e,v,[t_{min},t_{max}])$	
	$\mathcal{C}_{1v-1e}$	$\mathcal{C}_{1(e,t)-1v}$	**AUC**	**F1**	**AUC**	**F1**
TRUTHFINDER		✗	0.0006	0.0012	0.0006	0.0012
LTM	✗	✗	0.1319	0.0199	0.2030	0.0218
LTM	✗	✓	0.0212	0.0505	0.0407	0.0793
TRUEPIE	✓	✗	0.0587	0.1430	0.0587	0.1430
MAJVOTE	✗	✓	0.3336	0.4318	0.4958	0.5927
TFWIN	✓	✓	0.4746	0.6361	0.5523	0.6489
Ours (PGMCC)	✗	✓	0.4840	0.6502	0.6006	0.7254
Ours (PGMCC)	✓	✓	**0.4987**	**0.6634**	**0.6075**	**0.7316**

• TRUEPIE (Li et al., 2018): It was a bootstrapping method using $\mathcal{C}_{1(v)-1e}$ and estimating pattern reliability.
• MAJVOTE (Goldman and Warmuth, 1995): It used the weighted majority voting strategy and returned the most frequent temporal fact.
• TFWIN (Wang et al., 2019): It was the state-of-the-art bootstrapping method for truth discovery on fact extraction. However, error propagation is serious in its iterative process.

4.2.2 Evaluation settings

All the methods can only find truth of temporal fact at one time point, e.g., (French, Jacques Chirac, 1995). However, due to the incompleteness of fact description in data, some time points of temporal facts could be missing. One way to improve the evaluation is to composite true temporal fact time points $\{e, v, t\}$ into temporal fact time period $\{e, v, [t_{min}, t_{max}]\}$. We evaluate the performance on both temporal fact time point $\{e, v, t\}$ and temporal fact time period $\{e, v, [t_{min}, t_{max}]\}$. To evaluate on time period $\{e, v, [t_{min}, t_{max}]\}$, we look at every single time points (e, v, t) in the period $(t \in [t_{min}, t_{max}])$.

4.2.3 Evaluation metrics

We evaluate all competitive methods using *precision, recall, F1 score*, and *AUC* (Area Under the Curve). Precision is the the fraction of temporal fact truth among all the temporal fact that were labelled as true. Recall is the fraction of true temporal facts our approach finds among the ground truth temporal facts. F1 score is the harmonic mean of precision and recall. For all of the metrics, higher score indicates that the method performs better.

4.3 Effectiveness

The results are given in Table 2. Our proposed method PGMCC consistently outperforms all the baselines on finding (country, president, time)-facts (i.e., presidential terms).

PGMCC vs LTM: PGMCC performs significantly better than LTM (+34.5% AUC; +64.4% F1) on evaluating time points, and performs better with (+40.45% AUC; +71.2% F1) on evaluating time periods. LTM was designed to solve structured truth finding like the bookseller example. So, there were many conflicts when applied to temporal fact extraction. PGMCC has multi-constraint as observable variables to alleviate the issue.

PGMCC vs TFWIN: PGMCC performs better than TFWIN (+2.4% AUC; +2.8% F1) on evaluating time points, and performs better with (+5.2% AUC; +8.3% F1) on evaluating time periods. TFWIN started with seed patterns and defined constraints as a rule to eliminate conflicting tuples. However, the inference on conflicts was based on local information (i.e., the current pattern reliability estimation). During this process, error might propagate through iterations. PGMCC is a probabilistic graphical model that can avoid error propagation by modeling constraints as variables and inferring truth with the global data distributions.

PGMCC with different constraints: See the last two rows in Table 2. For both PGMCC and TFWIN models, a complete constraint set, i.e., $\{\mathcal{C}_{1(v)-1e}$ and $\mathcal{C}_{1(e,t)-1v}\}$, gives the best performance. Partial constraint cannot fully identify conflicts or false tuples. $\mathcal{C}_{1(e,t)-1v}$ plays a significant role in extracting *country's president*.

Table 3: Pattern's reliability for country's presidency.

Textual Pattern p	$r_{p(post)}$	$r_{p(tag)}$
president `Person` of `Country`	0.920	0.870
`Country`'s current president `Person`,	0.978	0.250
`Country`'s newly elected president , `Person` ,	0.970	0.030
`Person`, now president of `Country`,	0.750	0.110
`Person`, who has ruled `Country`	0.438	0.994
$COUNTRY's former president `Person`	0.113	0.994
`Person`, who ruled `Country`	0.607	0.758
`Country` president `Person` signed	0.553	0.327
`Country` premier `Person`	0.012	0.010
`Country` foreign minister `Person`	0	0
`Country` golfer `Person`	0	0

4.4 Pattern Source Reliability Analysis

Table 3 presented some pattern examples and their scores. Here are our observations. First, the pattern "president `Person` of `Country`" is the only pattern that shows high reliability on both types of time signals (above 0.85). Second, the textual patterns that describe the current presidency are likely to have higher reliability on *text gen. time* than *temporal tag*, because the presidency was likely to be in the same time as the document was generated. These patterns usually have words such as "current", "newly", and "now". Third, the textual patterns that describe the past presidency are likely to have higher reliability on "tag" than "post", because the presidency was likely to be in the same time as the event (described in the sentence) happened but before the time of the document being generated. These patterns usually have words such as "have governed", "have ruled", "former", and "formerly".

5 Related Work

In this section, we review two relevant fields to our work, temporal fact extraction and truth discovery.

5.1 Truth Discovery

In big data era, the issue of "Veracity" on resolving conflicts among multi-source information is quite serious (Berti-Equille, 2015; Vydiswaran et al., 2011; Waguih and Berti-Equille, 2014; Dong et al., 2009; Galland et al., 2010; Xiao et al., 2016; Yin and Tan, 2011). Truth discovery methods find trustworthy information from conflicting multi-source (Xiao et al., 2015; Li et al., 2015). Several truth discovery methods have been proposed for various scenarios, and they have been successfully applied in diverse application domains. A few truth discovery methods are probabilistic model. LTM solved the "`Book`'s `author` list problem" and modeled its source in two-fold quality (Zhao et al., 2012). GTM solved the task of finding true numeric value of "New York City's population" (Zhao and Han, 2012). TEXTTRUTH found the true answer for a question from multi users (Zhang et al., 2018b).

5.2 Temporal Fact Extraction

Temporal fact extraction is to extract (entity, attribute name, attribute value)-tuples along with their time conditions from text corpora (Sil and Cucerzan, 2014; Hoang-Vu et al., 2016; Chekol, 2017; Zhang et al., 2018a; Shang et al., 2018; Zeng et al., 2019; Jiang et al., 2019). Textual patterns have been proposed to extract structured data from unstructured text data in an unsupervised way, such as E-A patterns (Gupta et al., 2014), parsing patterns (Nakashole et al., 2012), and meta patterns (Jiang et al., 2017). However, patterns are of different reliability and extractions are sometimes conflicting. In order to get reliable temporal fact, we addressed this problem using truth discovery.

6 Limitations and Future Work

Though the proposed approach show effectiveness in experiments, it and/or the study has several limitations. First of all, because collecting *temporal* factual truth for a variety of attributes is very expensive, in this study, we only studied a single relation type. In future work, we will apply the approach to other types of temporal-facts if correct constraints can be defined, such as sports team's players and spouse relationship. Second, though the patterns were generated by automated mining technologies such as Meta Patterns (Jiang et al., 2017) (in other words, they are not hand-crafted), the pattern mining as a preprocessing step is needed. The approach is not end-to-end.

7 Conclusions

In this work, we proposed a probabilistic graphical model for inferring true facts and pattern reliability. It had two novel designs for temporal facts: (1) it modeled pattern reliability on temporal tag in text and text generation time; (2) it modeled commonsense constraints as observable variables. Experimental results demonstrated that our model outperformed existing methods.

Acknowledgements

This work was supported by NSF Grant IIS-1849816 and CCF-1901059.

References

Laure Berti-Equille. 2015. Data veracity estimation with ensembling truth discovery methods. In *Big Data (Big Data), 2015 IEEE International Conference on*, pages 2628–2636. IEEE.

Melisachew Wudage Chekol. 2017. Scaling probabilistic temporal query evaluation. In *Proceedings of the 2017 ACM on Conference on Information and Knowledge Management*, pages 697–706. ACM.

Luciano Del Corro, Abdalghani Abujabal, Rainer Gemulla, and Gerhard Weikum. 2015. Finet: Context-aware fine-grained named entity typing. In *Proceedings of the 2015 Conference on Empirical Methods in Natural Language Processing*, pages 868–878.

Xin Luna Dong, Laure Berti-Equille, and Divesh Srivastava. 2009. Integrating conflicting data: the role of source dependence. *Proceedings of the VLDB Endowment*, 2(1):550–561.

Alban Galland, Serge Abiteboul, Amélie Marian, and Pierre Senellart. 2010. Corroborating information from disagreeing views. In *Proceedings of the third ACM international conference on Web search and data mining*, pages 131–140. ACM.

Sally A Goldman and Manfred K Warmuth. 1995. Learning binary relations using weighted majority voting. *Machine Learning*, 20(3):245–271.

Rahul Gupta, Alon Halevy, Xuezhi Wang, Steven Euijong Whang, and Fei Wu. 2014. Biperpedia: An ontology for search applications. *Proceedings of the VLDB Endowment*, 7(7):505–516.

Tuan-Anh Hoang-Vu, Huy T Vo, and Juliana Freire. 2016. A unified index for spatio-temporal keyword queries. In *Proceedings of the 25th ACM International on Conference on Information and Knowledge Management*, pages 135–144. ACM.

Meng Jiang, Jingbo Shang, Taylor Cassidy, Xiang Ren, Lance M Kaplan, Timothy P Hanratty, and Jiawei Han. 2017. Metapad: Meta pattern discovery from massive text corpora. In *Proceedings of the 23rd ACM SIGKDD International Conference on Knowledge Discovery and Data Mining*, pages 877–886. ACM.

Tianwen Jiang, Tong Zhao, Bing Qin, Ting Liu, Nitesh V Chawla, and Meng Jiang. 2019. The role of" condition" a novel scientific knowledge graph representation and construction model. In *Proceedings of the 25th ACM SIGKDD International Conference on Knowledge Discovery & Data Mining*, pages 1634–1642.

Qi Li, Meng Jiang, Xikun Zhang, Meng Qu, Timothy P Hanratty, Jing Gao, and Jiawei Han. 2018. Truepie: Discovering reliable patterns in pattern-based information extraction. In *Proceedings of the 24th ACM SIGKDD International Conference on Knowledge Discovery & Data Mining*, pages 1675–1684. ACM.

Yaliang Li, Qi Li, Jing Gao, Lu Su, Bo Zhao, Wei Fan, and Jiawei Han. 2015. On the discovery of evolving truth. In *Proceedings of the 21th ACM SIGKDD International Conference on Knowledge Discovery and Data Mining*, pages 675–684. ACM.

Ndapandula Nakashole, Gerhard Weikum, and Fabian Suchanek. 2012. Patty: a taxonomy of relational patterns with semantic types. In *Proceedings of the 2012 Joint Conference on Empirical Methods in Natural Language Processing and Computational Natural Language Learning*, pages 1135–1145. Association for Computational Linguistics.

Nils Reimers, Nazanin Dehghani, and Iryna Gurevych. 2016. Temporal anchoring of events for the timebank corpus. In *Proceedings of the 54th Annual Meeting of the Association for Computational Linguistics (Volume 1: Long Papers)*, volume 1, pages 2195–2204.

Jingbo Shang, Jialu Liu, Meng Jiang, Xiang Ren, Clare R Voss, and Jiawei Han. 2018. Automated phrase mining from massive text corpora. *IEEE Transactions on Knowledge and Data Engineering*, 30(10):1825–1837.

Avirup Sil and Silviu-Petru Cucerzan. 2014. Towards temporal scoping of relational facts based on wikipedia data. In *Proceedings of the Eighteenth Conference on Computational Natural Language Learning*, pages 109–118.

VG Vydiswaran, ChengXiang Zhai, and Dan Roth. 2011. Content-driven trust propagation framework. In *Proceedings of the 17th ACM SIGKDD international conference on Knowledge discovery and data mining*, pages 974–982. ACM.

Dalia Attia Waguih and Laure Berti-Equille. 2014. Truth discovery algorithms: An experimental evaluation. *arXiv:1409.6428*.

Xueying Wang, Haiqiao Zhang, Qi Li, Yiyu Shi, and Meng Jiang. 2019. A novel unsupervised approach for precise temporal slot filling from incomplete and noisy temporal contexts. In *The World Wide Web Conference*, pages 3328–3334. ACM.

Houping Xiao, Jing Gao, Qi Li, Fenglong Ma, Lu Su, Yunlong Feng, and Aidong Zhang. 2016. Towards confidence in the truth: A bootstrapping based truth discovery approach. In *Proceedings of the 22nd ACM SIGKDD International Conference on Knowledge Discovery and Data Mining*, pages 1935–1944. ACM.

Houping Xiao, Yaliang Li, Jing Gao, Fei Wang, Liang Ge, Wei Fan, Long H Vu, and Deepak S Turaga. 2015. Believe it today or tomorrow? detecting untrustworthy information from dynamic multi-source data. In *Proceedings of the 2015 SIAM International Conference on Data Mining*, pages 397–405. SIAM.

Xiaoxin Yin, Jiawei Han, and S Yu Philip. 2008. Truth discovery with multiple conflicting information providers on the web. *IEEE Transactions on Knowledge and Data Engineering*, 20(6):796–808.

Xiaoxin Yin and Wenzhao Tan. 2011. Semi-supervised truth discovery. In *Proceedings of the 20th international conference on World wide web*, pages 217–226. ACM.

Qingkai Zeng, Mengxia Yu, Wenhao Yu, Jinjun Xiong, Yiyu Shi, and Meng Jiang. 2019. Faceted hierarchy: A new graph type to organize scientific concepts and a construction method. In *Proceedings of the Thirteenth Workshop on Graph-Based Methods for Natural Language Processing (TextGraphs-13)*, pages 140–150.

Chao Zhang, Fangbo Tao, Xiusi Chen, Jiaming Shen, Meng Jiang, Brian Sadler, Michelle Vanni, and Jiawei Han. 2018a. Taxogen: Constructing topical concept taxonomy by adaptive term embedding and clustering. In *Proceedings of the 24th ACM SIGKDD International Conference on Knowledge Discovery & Data Mining*.

Hengtong Zhang, Yaliang Li, Fenglong Ma, Jing Gao, and Lu Su. 2018b. Texttruth: an unsupervised approach to discover trustworthy information from multi-sourced text data. In *Proceedings of the 24th ACM SIGKDD International Conference on Knowledge Discovery & Data Mining*, pages 2729–2737. ACM.

Bo Zhao and Jiawei Han. 2012. A probabilistic model for estimating real-valued truth from conflicting sources. *Proc. of QDB*.

Bo Zhao, Benjamin IP Rubinstein, Jim Gemmell, and Jiawei Han. 2012. A bayesian approach to discovering truth from conflicting sources for data integration. *Proceedings of the VLDB Endowment*, 5(6):550–561.

Developing a How-to Tip Machine Comprehension Dataset and its Evaluation in Machine Comprehension by BERT

Tengyang Chen[†], **Hongyu Li**[†], **Miho Kasamatsu**[†], **Takehito Utsuro**[†], **Yasuhide Kawada**[‡]
[†]Graduate School of Systems and Information Engineering, University of Tsukuba, Japan
[‡]Logworks Co., Ltd., Japan

Abstract

In the field of factoid question answering (QA), it is known that the state-of-the-art technology has achieved an accuracy comparable to that of humans in a certain benchmark challenge. On the other hand, in the area of non-factoid QA, there is still a limited number of datasets for training QA models, i.e., machine comprehension models. Considering such a situation within the field of the non-factoid QA, this paper aims to develop a dataset for training Japanese how-to tip QA models. This paper applies one of the state-of-the-art machine comprehension models to the Japanese how-to tip QA dataset. The trained how-to tip QA model is also compared with a factoid QA model trained with a Japanese factoid QA dataset. Evaluation results revealed that the how-to tip machine comprehension performance was almost comparative with that of the factoid machine comprehension even with the training data size reduced to around 4% of the factoid machine comprehension. Thus, the how-to tip machine comprehension task requires much less training data compared with the factoid machine comprehension task.

1 Introduction

Recent advances in the field of QA or machine comprehension are mostly in the domain of factoid QA related to Wikipedia articles and news articles (Yi et al., 2015; Pranav et al., 2016, 2018). One of the most well-known QA datasets and benchmark tests is the Stanford Question Answering Dataset (SQuAD) (Pranav et al., 2016, 2018), which is a reading comprehension dataset, consisting of questions posed by crowdworkers on a set of Wikipedia articles, where the answer to every question is a text segment, or span, from the corresponding reading passage, or the question might be unanswerable. It is reported[1] that state-of-the-art machine comprehension models trained with SQuAD outperform humans (Devlin et al., 2019; Zhang et al., 2019).

However, apart from the issues related to developing benchmark datasets for factoid QA and improving state-of-the-art general-purpose machine comprehension models, there is a relatively limited number of published literature that handles issues, such as the development of datasets for non-factoid QA and the application of state-of-the-art general-purpose machine comprehension models to those non-factoid datasets. Typical non-factoid QA tasks include opinion QA, definition QA, reason QA, and how-to tip QA.

Among various kinds of non-factoid knowledge which are the key to developing techniques for non-factoid QA tasks, a recent study (Ohkawa et al., 2018) examined the types of Japanese websites which include various how-to tips related to job hunting, marriage, and apartment. The study (Ohkawa et al., 2018) also aims to automatically identify those how-to tip websites, which will be an important knowledge source for training how-to tip QA models. Considering such a situation, within the field of non-factoid QA, this paper studies how to develop a dataset for training Japanese how-to tip (hereafter throughout the paper, we use the simplified term "tip") QA models. As examples in this paper, we developed tip QA datasets for 'job hunting," "marriage," "apartment," "hay fever," "dentist," and "food poisoning," where "job hunting" and "marriage" tip QAs are for both training and testing, while other tip QAs are only for testing. For "job hunting", Figure 1 presents a typical example of a tuple of a context, a tip question, and an answer. Furthermore, in order to understand rough idea of

[1] https://rajpurkar.github.io/SQuAD-explorer/

Proceedings of the Third Workshop on Fact Extraction and VERification (FEVER), pages 26–35
July 9, 2020.

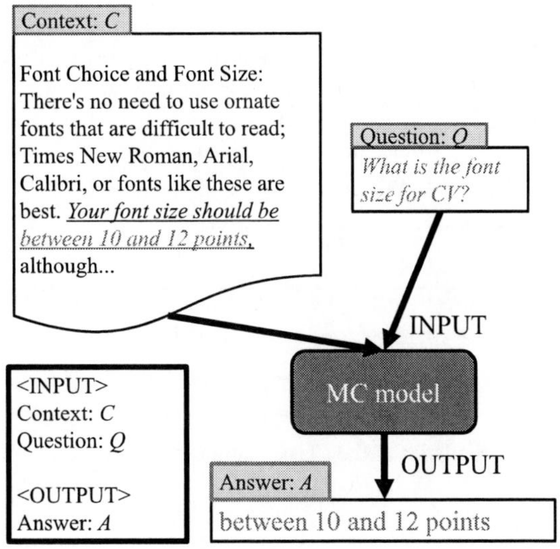

Figure 1: An example of the machine comprehension model of tip QA for "job hunting" together with an example of a tuple of a context C, a question Q, and answer A (extracted from a column web page entitled "Formatting Tips for Your Curriculum Vitae (CV)" (`https://www.thebalancecareers.com/curriculum-vitae-format-2060351`) from a tip website titled "The Balance Careers" (`https://www.thebalancecareers.com/`))

the (how-to) tip questions we study in this paper in the broader sense, we manually classify them into five types as shown in Table 1 and also shown several examples for each of the five types and their statistics within the dataset we developed in this paper.

This paper then applies BERT (Devlin et al., 2019), one of the state-of-the-art machine comprehension models, to a Japanese tip QA dataset. The trained tip QA model is also compared with a factoid QA model which is also trained with a Japanese factoid QA dataset. Evaluation results revealed that the tip machine comprehension performance was almost comparative with that of the factoid machine comprehension even with the training data size reduced to around 4% of the factoid machine comprehension. Thus, the tip machine comprehension task requires much less training data compared with the factoid machine comprehension task.

2 Query Focuses and Collecting Web Pages

This section briefly describes the workflow of collecting web pages. First, the notion of *query focus* is a keyword used for every search request related to a specific subject. For example, whenever the aim was to collect web pages about anything related to job hunting, the word "job hunting" was always put at the beginning of the query, and all available suggested keywords provided by the search engine were collected, such as "job hunting self-promotion" and "job hunting portfolio." Using all such suggested keywords as queries (called *search engine suggests* or *suggests*), the search engine is crawled, and top 10 results for each suggest are collected.

2.1 Collecting Search Engine Suggests

Web search engine suggests are the query keywords automatically offered by a search engine when a user types part of a search query. Such suggested keywords can be seen as frequent user activities logged by the search engine, and they mostly lead to pages on trending topics. For a given query focus keyword, about 100 specified types of Japanese hiragana characters were entered into Google ® search engine from which up to 1,000 suggests were collected. These 100 types of Japanese hiragana characters include the Japanese alphabet consisting of 50 characters, voiced and semi-voiced variants of voiceless characters and Youon.

tip question type	examples	rate (%)
essential, words of caution, reminder	what is the essential of $\sim$? / what are the words of caution on $\sim$? / what should one take care of when $\sim$?	23.6
characteristics, definition, knowledge, fact, rule	what is the characteristics of $\sim$? / what is $\sim$? / which documents are required to submit to the city hall when $\sim$?	18.5
method and how-to tip (in the narrower sense)	how can I do $\sim$? / what is the tip, know-how, hack for doing $\sim$?	16.6
reason, cause, background, purpose	what is the reason for $\sim$? / why $\sim$? / what is the purpose of $\sim$?	4.3
habit, experience, recommendation (tip of any type other than the above four types)	what is the recommendation when $\sim$? / what should I use when $\sim$? / when should I start $\sim$?	37.0
total	—	100

Table 1: Statistics of the Classification of Tip Question Types

2.2 Collecting Web Pages

Google Custom Search API[2] was used to scrape web pages from the search engine. Using the web search engine suggests collected in the previous section combined with the query focus keyword as queries (in the form of AND search), the first 10 pages returned per search query are collected. The set of web pages queried by suggest s can be represented as $D(s, N)$, where N is 10 as a constant standing for top N pages. Additionally, the search engine suggests were saved for every web page. Since different search engine suggests could lead to the same web page, one web page could have multiple suggests. Let S be the set of all suggests about one query focus. Then, the set of web pages scraped using all possible suggests is represented as D.

$$D = \bigcup_{s \in S} D(s, N)$$

3 Selecting Candidates of Tip Websites

This paper employs LDA (latent Dirichlet allocation) (Blei et al., 2003) to model topic distributions among documents. Let D be a document set containing all collected web pages and K (= 50 in this paper) be the number of topics. When the topic model is applied, topic distribution $P(z_n \mid d)$ is available for every d ($d \in D$). Every document d is assigned a topic with the highest probability among all its $P(z_n \mid d)$. The net effect is that for every topic z_n, there is a group $D(z_n)$ ($n = 1, \ldots, K$) of corresponding documents that are assigned to z_n.

[2] https://developers.google.com/custom-search/

Then, domain names are extracted from all collected web pages based on their URLs. The domain names that have corresponding web pages reside in 10 or more sets $D(z_n)$ ($n = 1, \ldots, K$), i.e., they have their web pages under more than or equal to 10 topics which are considered as candidates for tip websites[3]. Out of those candidates whose numbers are 31 for job-hunting in this experiment, 14 domain names were randomly selected, for all of which tip QAs were successfully collected. Henceforth, the set of those 14 tips websites will be denoted as T. Similarly, for marriage, 13 domain names have their web pages under more than or equal to 10 topics and are considered as candidates for tip websites. For all of those 13 domain names, tip QAs were successfully collected. Thus, for marriage, the set of those 13 tips websites will be denoted as T.

4 Collecting Tip QAs

4.1 Collecting Web Pages of Tip Websites

From each website out of the set T of tip websites, web pages are collected as the source for collecting tip QAs. First, from each website of T, all of its web pages are collected into set $D^{\text{inf}}(T)$. Then, the LDA topic model (Blei et al., 2003) $P(z_n \mid d)$ (available for every d ($d \in D$)) trained in Sec-

[3] Ohkawa et al. (2018) examined quantitative characteristics of tip websites. Furthermore, it is reported in Ohkawa et al. (2018) that domain names of candidate tip websites can be collected from those that have corresponding web pages in sets $D(z_n)$ of web pages for multiple topics z_n ($n = 1, \ldots, K$). It is observed, however, that typical tip websites actually have their web pages under far more than two topics and typically, more than or equal to 10 topics. Thus, in this paper, it was decided to select domain names which have their web pages under more than or equal to 10 topics as candidates for tip websites.

# Pairs of question and answer	1	2	3	4	5	Total
# Web pages (%)	131 (28.1)	102 (21.9)	64 (13.7)	33 (7.1)	136 (29.2)	466 (100)

Table 2: # Pairs of QA collected from a web page (for "job hunting" and "marriage")

tion 3 with the set D of web pages scraped using all possible suggests is applied to each web page d within set $D^{\mathrm{inf}}(T)$. According to the probability distribution $P(z_n|d)$ of topics z_n $(n = 1, \ldots, K)$ for each web page d, the topic z_n with the highest probability is assigned to d. Then, the set of web pages to which the topic z_n is assigned is denoted as $D^{\mathrm{inf}}(z_n, T)$:

$$D^{\mathrm{inf}}(z_n, T) = \left\{ d \in D^{\mathrm{inf}}(T) \;\middle|\; z_n = \underset{z_u\ (u=1,\ldots,K)}{\mathrm{argmax}} \ P(z_u|d) \right\}$$

For the query focus "job hunting," out of the total $K = 50$ topics, $|D^{\mathrm{inf}}(z_n, T)| > 0$ holds, i.e., at least one web page is assigned to 42 topics for job hunting and 29 for marriage.

4.2 "Column Pages" as the Source for Collecting Tip QAs

This study analyzes the types of web pages which tend to include more and more tips compared with other types of web pages. This paper examines tip websites which include column pages containing various tips and also include other types of web pages, such as pages for commercial sale of products or pages with reviews and experiences. However, most tips are found only in column pages but not in other types of pages. The type of web pages which tend to include tips are mostly column pages.

Out of the set $D^{\mathrm{inf}}(z_n, T)$ of web pages defined in the previous section, all the column pages are extracted into a subset:

$$D_c^{\mathrm{inf}}(z_n, T)$$

In the case of the query focus "job hunting," out of 42 topics satisfying $|D^{\mathrm{inf}}(z_n, T)| > 0$, 36 topics satisfy $|D_c^{\mathrm{inf}}(z_n, T)| > 0$, i.e., include column pages. For "marriage", all the 29 topics satisfy $|D_c^{\mathrm{inf}}(z_n, T)| > 0$. For each topic z_n, all the web pages in this set are used as a source for collecting tip QAs.

4.3 Procedure for Collecting Tip QAs

This section describes the procedure for collecting tip questions and examples, such as those presented in Figure 1. From each web page within the set $D_c^{\mathrm{inf}}(z_n, T)$ constructed in the previous section, tuples of context C, question Q, and answer A are manually collected. Specifically, within each column web page, every paragraph is examined, and it is decided whether a pair of a question and an answer can be collected from the paragraph. From each column web page, at most 5 pairs of a question and an answer are collected. Figure 1 presents an example of collecting a tuple of a context, a question, and an answer from a column web page of a "job hunting" tip website. In this example, context C, the following paragraph about font choice and font size is selected:

> There's no need to use ornate fonts that are difficult to read; ... Your font size should be between 10 and 12 points, although ...

From this paragraph, a pair of question Q "What is the font size for CV?" and answer A "between 10 and 12 points" is extracted. Table 2 lists the distribution of the number of the pairs of a question and an answer collected from a web page for "job hunting" and "marriage".

For the query focus "job hunting," out of the overall 1,268 column web pages collected following the procedure of this paper, 352 pages were actually examined, out of which 907 pairs of tip QAs are collected. For the query focus "marriage," out of the overall 3,075 column web pages collected following the procedure of this paper, 114 pages were actually examined, out of which 432 pairs of tip QAs are collected. For "apartment" query focuses, 50 pairs of tip QAs are collected. For other query focuses "hay fever," "dentist," and "food poisoning," a total of 50 pairs of tip QAs are collected. Table 3 presents an example of Japanese tip QAs for each of "job hunting," "marriage," and "hay fever." These numbers and examples are all for SQuAD1.1 type answerable questions only.

Context C	Question Q	Answer A
履歴書に短所を書く時は前向きにまとめるようにします.「工夫して克服した」「直すように努力している」などと書けば悪いイメージの短所で好印象を与えることも可能です. 自分の短所の中で努力すれば改善しそうなものを選ぶと書きやすいでしょう.	履歴書に短所を書く時のポイントは? (What is the tip when including one's weak points into one's resume?)	前向きにまとめる (Organize them positively.)
一年の中でも結婚式の費用を抑えやすく比較的安い月といえるのが1月・2月. 寒さが厳しいシーズンであるため, 結婚式の施行数もそれほど多くなく, 通常よりも割安なプランを用意している会場が多数あります. また, 希望の日程で日取りを抑えやすいのも魅力. キャンドルの炎を使ったやさしい光のライトアップやキラキラと輝く装飾など, 冬らしいコーディネートを取り入れるのもオススメです.	一年の中でも結婚式の費用を抑えやすく比較的安い月は? (In which month, is it the easiest to save money for a wedding?)	1月・2月 (January and February)
そのため花粉の季節は, 室内の湿度を 50∼55%ほどに保てるように加湿器を使用しましょう.	花粉の季節に保つべき室内の湿度の目安は? (How much indoor humidity should be maintained in the pollen season?)	50∼55% (50∼55%)

Table 3: Examples of Japanese tip QAs selected from training and test datasets used in evaluation (tuples of Context C, Question Q, and Answer A for query focuses "job hunting," "marriage," and "hay fever", for SQuAD1.1: answerable questions)

From these tip QAs of SQuAD1.1 type with answerable questions, tip QAs of SQuAD2.0 type with unanswerable questions are manually created. From a tuple of a context C, a question Q, and an answer A of SQuAD1.1 type, which is answerable in that the context C includes the answer A to the question Q, the annotator manually created another tuple, which is an unanswerable QA, of a context C' ($\neq C$), a question Q' ($= Q$), and the answer $A' = \langle\text{null}\rangle$. Here, within exactly the same column web page of the tip website, from which the context C is extracted, the annotator searched for another paragraph other than C, which does not include any answer to the original question Q. The selected paragraph C' constitutes the context of a tip QA of SQuAD2.0 type with an unanswerable question. Note that it is quite important to search for C' within exactly the same column web page of the tip website, from which the context C is extracted. For example, in the case of the tip QA on "job hunting" in Figure 1, for the question Q "What is the font size for CV?", within the same column web page about "job hunting", another paragraph C' other than C is selected. The selected paragraph C' still presents a certain tip about job hunting and CV, while it does not include any tip about the font size for CV. We follow this strategy simply because it avoids tip QAs with unanswerable questions becoming much easier to answer compared with tip QAs with answerable questions. With this strategy, for each of almost all the tip QAs of SQuAD1.1 type answerable questions, we successfully created at least one tip QA of SQuAD2.0 type with an unanswerable question.

5 Applying BERT to Tip Machine Comprehension

5.1 Dataset for Evaluation

In this paper, we developed two types of datasets for evaluation: one for SQuAD1.1 type answerable questions only and another for SQuAD2.0 type answerable and unanswerable questions. This paper presents evaluation results with the SQuAD2.0 type dataset. For the SQuAD2.0 type dataset, Table 4 presents the statistics of training and test datasets for evaluation in this paper. Table 4 (a) presents those of the training and test datasets for Japanese factoid QAs[4]. Those Japanese factoid QAs, which are of SQuAD2.0 type, are manually collected from Japanese quiz data by automatically identifying context texts from Japanese version of Wikipedia and then manually judging whether each identified context includes the answer to the question. Table 4 (b) and Table 4 (c) present the statistics of training and test datasets for Japanese tip QAs about "job hunting" and "marriage". Similarly, Table 4 (d) presents those for test datasets for Japanese tip QAs about "apartment," "hay fever," "dentist," and "food poisoning"[5].

[4] http://www.cl.ecei.tohoku.ac.jp/rcqa/ (in Japanese)

[5] Four annotators participated in the procedure of collecting tip QAs, where we measured inter-annotator agreement rate according to AC_1 (Gwet, 2008), but not to kappa (Cohen, 1960), mainly because two or more annotators tend to have high overall agreement rate, causing imbalanced class label distribution and instability of kappa. AC_1 inter-annotator agreement is measured through the two sub-procedures: i.e., i) manually judging whether the questions selected by two out of three annotators are semantically equivalent when exactly the same context paragraph is given to the three anno-

(a) Factoid QAs

	# tuples of a context, a question and an answer (answerable / unanswerable)	average # words within a context	average # words of a question
Train.	27,645/28,906	88.2	26.1
Test	49/51	82.8	27.1

(b) Tip QAs: "job hunting"

	# tuples of a context, a question and an answer (answerable / unanswerable)	average # words within a context	average # words of a question
Train.	755/845	63.0	10.7
Test	50/54	71.3	9.7

(c) Tip QAs: "marriage"

	# tuples of a context, a question and an answer (answerable / unanswerable)	average # words within a context	average # words of a question
Train.	382/382	44.2	11.2
Test	50/48	68.7	10.2

(d) Tip QAs: "apartment," "hay fever," "dentist," and "food poisoning"

query focus	# tuples of a context, a question and an answer (answerable / unanswerable)	average # words within a context	average # words of a question
apartment	50/49	82.0	10.3
hay fever, dentist, food poisoning	50/43	71.0	9.5

Table 4: Statistics of training and test datasets

5.2 BERT Implementation

As the version of BERT (Devlin et al., 2019) implementation which can handle a text in Japanese, the TensorFlow version[6] and the Multilingual Cased model[7] were used as the pre-trained model. Before applying BERT modules, MeCab[8] was applied with IPAdic dictionary, and the Japanese text was segmented into a morpheme sequence. Then, within the BERT fine-tuning module, the WordPiece module with 110k shared WordPiece vocabulary was applied, and the Japanese text was further segmented into a subword unit sequence. Finally, the BERT fine-tuning module for machine comprehension[9] was applied as well as the fine-tuned model. The BERT pre-trained model was fine-tuned with the following three types of train-

tators, and ii) manually judging whether the answers selected by two out of three annotators are semantically equivalent when exactly the same pair of a question and a context is given to the three annotators (their detailed procedures are omitted for space restriction). Average of AC_1 is 0.61 for the sub-procedure i) and 0.92 for the sub-procedure ii), which are sufficiently high.

[6] `https://github.com/google-research/bert`

[7] Trained with 104 languages, available from `https://github.com/google-research/bert/blob/master/multilingual.md`.

[8] `http://taku910.github.io/mecab/` (in Japanese)

[9] `run_squad.py`, with the number of epochs as 2, batch size as 8, and learning rate as 0.00003.

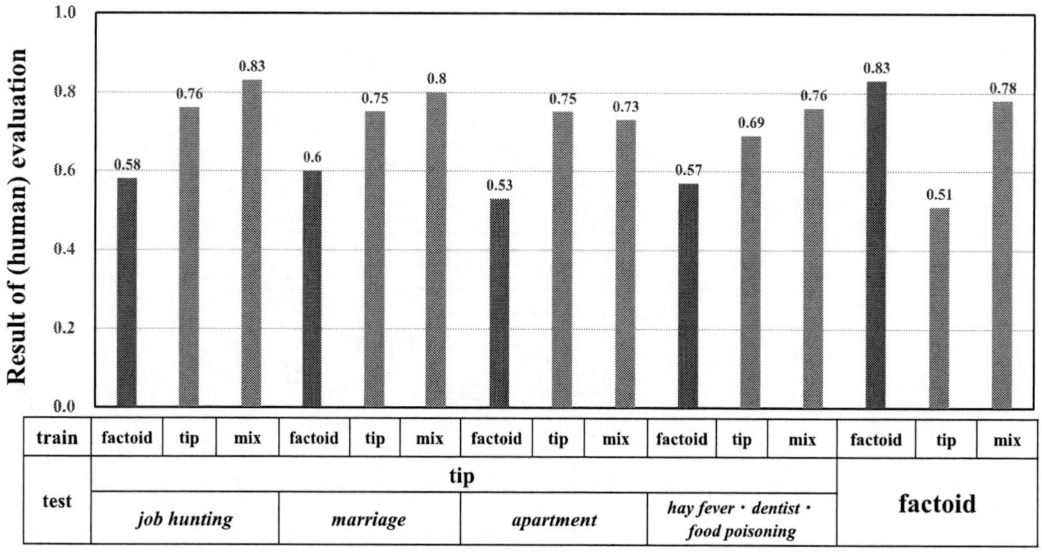

Figure 2: Evaluation results (exact match + partial match)

ing datasets:

(i) The training dataset of factoid QAs in Table 4 (a).

(ii) The training datasets of the tip QA about "job hunting" in Table 4 (b) and "marriage" in Table 4 (c).

(iii) Mix of (i) and (ii).

Here, note that we train a single model with each of these three training datasets (i)∼(iii), i.e., a single factoid machine comprehension model with (i), a single tip machine comprehension model with (ii), and a single machine comprehension model for the mixture of factoid and tip with (iii). It is especially important to note that we train a single tip machine comprehension model with the tip QA datasets about "job hunting" and "marriage", then evaluate it against the tip QA test datasets about all the query focuses, i.e., 'job hunting," "marriage," "apartment," "hay fever," "dentist," and "food poisoning."

5.3 Evaluation Result

In the evaluation, it is manually judged whether the answer predicted by the fine-tuned model and the reference answer partially match or not. We prefer manual evaluation rather than automatic evaluation, mainly because we prefer the quality of evaluation than avoiding the cost of evaluation. Figure 2 presents the evaluation results for the tip QA test datasets about "job hunting," "marriage," "apartment," and a mix of "hay fever," "dentist," and "food poisoning," as well as for the factoid QA test dataset. As clearly seen from these results, for all the tips test datasets, (ii) training only with tip QAs and (iii) training with a mix of tip QA and factoid QA training datasets outperforms and (i) training only with factoid QAs. For the factoid QA test datasets, on the other hand, (i) training only with factoid QAs and (iii) training with a mix of tip QA and factoid QA training datasets outperforms (ii) training only with tip QAs. This result supports the conclusion that the tip machine comprehension task is essentially different from the factoid machine comprehension task. But, still, for tips on "job hunting," "marriage," and the mix of "hay fever," "dentist," and "food poisoning," training with a mix of tip QA and factoid QA training datasets slightly outperforms training only with tip QAs. This result indicates that the tip machine comprehension task still to some extent benefits from a large-scale factoid QA training dataset when only small-scale tip QAs are available.

Another interesting finding is that, in tip machine comprehension, the single model fine-tuned with tip QA training datasets on "job hunting" and "marriage" performed well in tip machine comprehension of other query focuses, such as "apartment," "hay fever," "dentist," and "food poisoning." Thus, in tip comprehension, it is sufficient to collect tip QA only for one or two query fo-

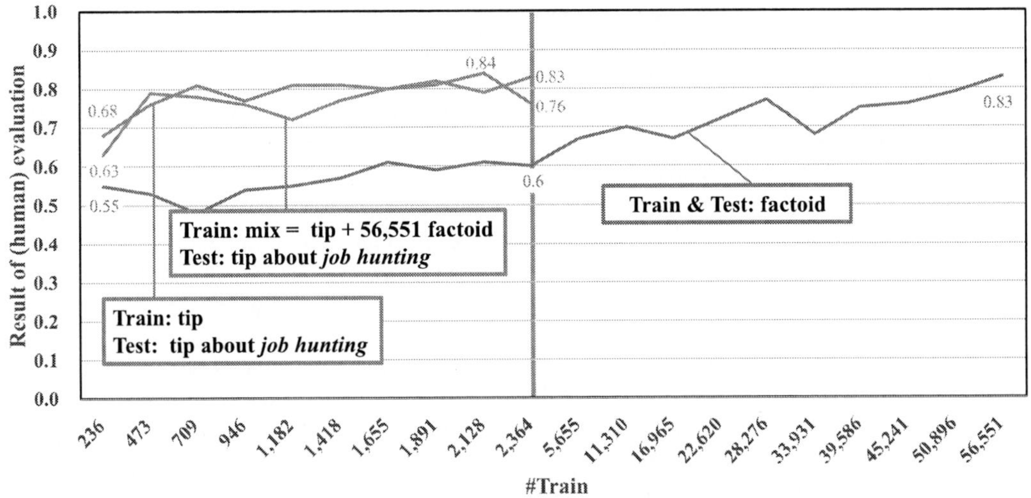

Figure 3: Comparing learning curves of factoid QAs, tip QAs, and training with a mix of factoid and tip QAs (exact match + partial match)

cuses, such as "job hunting" and "marriage," and then to fine-tune the tip machine comprehension model which is applicable to tip machine comprehension on any query focus.

Figure 3 also presents a comparison of learning curves for the following three cases:

(a) Training with 5%, 10%, ..., 95%, and 100% of factoid QA training dataset of (i) in the previous section and testing with the factoid QA test dataset from Table 4 (a) (plotted in blue).

(b) Training with 10%, 20%, ..., 90%, and 100% of the tip QA training datasets on "job hunting" and "marriage" of (ii) in the previous section and testing with the tip QA test dataset on "job hunting" of Table 4 (b) (plotted in orange).

(c) Training with a mix of (a) and (b), where the factoid QA training dataset of (a) is always with its 100% size, whereas the tip QA training dataset on "job hunting" of (b) has a size of 10%, 20%, ..., 90%, and 100% sizes and testing with the tip QA test dataset on "job hunting" of Table 4 (b) (plotted in green).

As can be seen from these results, the learning curve (b) of tip QAs and that (c) of the mix of factoid and tip QAs perform comparatively well and outperform that of factoid QAs (a) in the range of around a few thousand training data size. This result indicates that, at least for tip machine comprehension of "job hunting", benefit from a large-scale factoid QA training dataset is very little. Far more important finding in this result is that the tip machine comprehension performance is almost comparative with that of the factoid machine comprehension even when trained with as little as around 4% (≒ 2,364/56,551) of the training data size of the factoid machine comprehension. Thus, it can be concluded that the tip machine comprehension task requires much less training data compared with the factoid machine comprehension task.

6 Related Work

In the field of developing QA datasets or machine comprehension datasets which may include non-factoid QAs, quite a limited number of datasets are publicly available in any language. In English, MS MARCO (Nguyen et al., 2016) has been developed using Bing's search logs and passages of retrieved web pages, which may include non-factoid QAs. Question types in MS MARCO are classified into *numeric, entity, location, person*, and *description (phrase)*. In Chinese, DuReader (He et al., 2018) has been developed using Baidu Search and Baidu Zhidao, which is a Chinese community-based QA site. DuReader's question types are classified into *entity, description*, and *yes-no* questions on *fact* or *opinion*. DuReader's QAs definitely include non-factoid ones. Another type of non-factoid QA dataset is NarrativeQA (Kočiský et al., 2018) dataset (in English), which contains questions created by editors based on summaries of movie scripts and books. In the case of the Japanese language QA dataset, there is quite a limited number of publicly available factoid QA datasets, and one of them was introduced in Section 5.1. There is no publicly available Japanese non-factoid QA dataset.

7 Conclusion

This paper explored a way to develop a dataset for training Japanese tip QA models, and it applied BERT (Devlin et al., 2019) to a Japanese tip QA dataset. Evaluation results revealed that the tip machine comprehension performance was almost comparative with that of the factoid machine comprehension even with the training data size reduced to around 4% of the factoid machine comprehension. Thus, the tip machine comprehension task requires much less training data compared with the factoid machine comprehension task.

Future direction of this work includes applying the proposed framework of tip machine comprehension to other languages, such as English and Chinese. In both languages, factoid QA datasets are publicly available (e.g., SQuAD (Pranav et al., 2016, 2018) for English and CMRC2018 (Cui et al., 2018) for Chinese), and it is quite attainable to train a factoid machine comprehension model by fine-tuning the BERT pre-trained model and then to directly apply the factoid machine comprehension model to the tip machine comprehension task. Actually, as a preliminary work, a Chinese factoid machine comprehension model is trained by fine-tuning the pre-trained Multilingual Cased model with CMRC2018 Chinese factoid QA dataset[10][11], and then applying it to 30 Chinese tip questions on "marriage" with context texts. As a result, around 50% accuracy for manual evaluation is achieved by exact and partial match, which is almost comparative to the performance achieved in the Japanese tip machine comprehension task reported in this paper. Thus, it is expected that extending the proposed framework of tip machine comprehension to other languages, such as English and Chinese, is quite straightforward.

Another future direction is to extending the proposed framework of tip machine comprehension to open domain tip machine comprehension. This extension is similar to the extension of existing factoid machine comprehension with Wikipedia texts' paragraphs as contexts to open domain machine comprehension with the whole Wikipedia articles (Chen et al., 2017). In the extended open domain tip machine comprehension framework, the document retriever module is realized based on the tip websites search and column web page collection architectures proposed in this paper. The document reader module can be easily realized by simply applying the tip machine comprehension model of this paper.

Another definitely important future direction should be to invent a technique of how to automate the procedure of collecting column web pages and generating the tuple of a context C, a question Q, and answer A. This task can be regarded as that of training a tip machine comprehension model from a noisy training dataset.

[10] https://hfl-rc.github.io/cmrc2018/english/

[11] https://github.com/ymcui/cmrc2018

References

D. M. Blei, A. Y. Ng, and M. I. Jordan. 2003. Latent Dirichlet allocation. *Journal of Machine Learning Research*, 3:993–1022.

D. Chen, A. Fisch, J. Weston, and A. Bordes. 2017. Reading Wikipedia to answer open-domain questions. In *Proc. 55th ACL*, pages 1870–1879.

J. Cohen. 1960. A Coefficient of Agreement for Nominal Scales. *Educational and Psychological Measurement*, 20(1):37–46.

Y. Cui, T. Liu, L. Xiao, Z. Chen, W. Ma, W. Che, S. Wang, and G. Hu. 2018. A span-extraction dataset for Chinese machine reading comprehension. *CoRR*, abs/1810.07366.

J. Devlin, M.-W. Chang, K. Lee, and K. Toutanova. 2019. BERT: Pre-training of deep bidirectional transformers for language understanding. In *Proc. NAACL-HLT*, pages 4171–4186.

K. Gwet. 2008. Computing inter-rater reliability and its variance in the presence of high agreement. *The British Journal of Mathematical and Statistical Psychology*, 61:29–48.

W. He, K. Liu, J. Liu, Y. Lyu, S. Zhao, X. Xiao, Y. Liu, Y. Wang, H. Wu, Q. She, X. Liu, T. Wu, and H. Wang. 2018. DuReader: a Chinese machine reading comprehension dataset from real-world applications. In *Proc. MRQA*, pages 37–46.

T. Kočiský, J. Schwarz, P. Blunsom, C. Dyer, K. M. Hermann, G. Melis, and E. Grefenstette. 2018. The NarrativeQA reading comprehension challenge.

Transactions of the Association for Computational Linguistics, 6:317–328.

T. Nguyen, M. Rosenberg, X. Song, J. Gao, S. Tiwary, R. Majumder, and L. Deng. 2016. MS MARCO: A human generated machine reading comprehension dataset. *CoRR*, abs/1611.09268.

Y. Ohkawa, S. Kawabata, C. Zhao, W. Niu, Y. Lin, T. Utsuro, and Y. Kawada. 2018. Identifying tips Web sites of a specific query based on search engine suggests and the topic distribution. In *Proc. 3rd ABCSS*, pages 4347–4353.

R. Pranav, Z. Jian, L. Konstantin, and L. Percy. 2016. SQuAD: 100,000+ questions for machine comprehension of text. In *Proc. EMNLP*, pages 2383–2392.

R. Pranav, J. Robin, and L. Percy. 2018. Know what you don't know: Unanswerable questions for SQuAD. In *Proc. 56th ACL*, pages 784–789.

Y. Yi, Y. Wen-tau, and M. Christopher. 2015. WikiQA: A challenge dataset for open-domain question answering. In *Proc. EMNLP*, pages 2013–2018.

Z. Zhang, Y. Wu, J. Zhou, S. Duan, and H. Zhao. 2019. SG-Net: Syntax-guided machine reading comprehension. *CoRR*, abs/1908.05147.

Language Models as Fact Checkers?

Nayeon Lee[1*] **Belinda Z. Li**[2] **Sinong Wang**[2]
Wen-Tau Yih[2] **Hao Ma**[2] **Madian Khabsa**[2]
[1]Hong Kong University of Science and Technology [2]Facebook AI
nayeon.lee@connect.ust.hk
{belindali,sinongwang,scottyih,haom,mkhabsa}@fb.com

Abstract

Recent work has suggested that language models (LMs) store both common-sense and factual knowledge learned from pre-training data. In this paper, we leverage this implicit knowledge to create an effective end-to-end fact checker using a *solely* a language model, without any external knowledge or explicit retrieval components. While previous work on extracting knowledge from LMs have focused on the task of open-domain question answering, to the best of our knowledge, this is the first work to examine the use of language models as *fact checkers*. In a closed-book setting, we show that our zero-shot LM approach outperforms a random baseline on the standard FEVER task, and that our finetuned LM compares favorably with standard baselines. Though we do not ultimately outperform methods which use explicit knowledge bases, we believe our exploration shows that this method is viable and has much room for exploration.

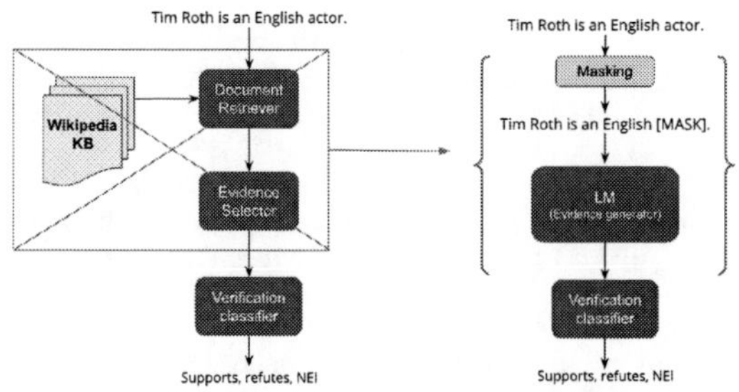

(a) Traditional fact-checking pipeline. (b) Our new fact-checking pipeline.

Figure 1: Traditional fact-checking pipeline (left) vs. Our LM-based pipeline (right)

1 Introduction

Pre-trained language models have recently lead to significant advancements in wide variety of NLP tasks, including question-answering, commonsense reasoning, and semantic relatedness (Devlin et al., 2018; Radford et al., 2019; Peters et al., 2018; Radford et al., 2018). These models are typically trained on documents mined from Wikipedia (among other websites). Recently, a number of works have found that LMs store a surprising amount of world knowledge, focusing particularly on the task of open-domain question answering (Petroni et al., 2019; Roberts et al., 2020). In this paper, we explore whether we can leverage the knowledge in LMs for *fact checking*.

We propose an approach (Fig. 1b) that replaces the document retriever and evidence selector models in traditional fact-checking (Fig. 1a) with a single language model that generates masked tokens. This offers a number of advantages over the traditional approach: first, the procedure is overall simpler, requiring fewer resources and computation – we do not need to maintain an explicit knowledge base external to our LM, and we do not need an explicit retrieval step. The latter in particular can lead to a huge speedup in the system, since we can skip the time-consuming step of searching over a potentially massive space of documents. Second, LMs are widely-available and are currently attracting significant research effort. Thus, research in language-modeling, particularly in improving LMs ability to memorizing knowledge, may also improve the overall effectiveness of our fact-checking pipeline. Lastly, our system further shifts the paradigm towards "one model for all" — LMs have been used for a wide variety of tasks, and now also for fact checking.

In order to determine the feasibility of our approach, we start with a human review study where participants are given a claim from FEVER (Thorne et al., 2018a), and are asked to validate the claim using only a BERT language model. We found that users had reasonable success in determining claim validity. Empowered by the results,

*Work done while at Facebook AI.

Proceedings of the Third Workshop on Fact Extraction and VERification (FEVER), pages 36–41
July 9, 2020.

we design an *end-to-end* neural approach for utilizing BERT as a fact checker (see Figure 1b). At a high level, we first generate an evidence sentence by masking the claim and using BERT to "fill in" the mask. We then feed the generated sentence, alongside the original claim, to a verification classifier model that classifies whether the claim is supported, refuted, or the information is insufficient to make a call.

The rest of the paper is organized as such: Section 2 gives an overview of the problem space. Section 3 describes our preliminary experiments. Sections 4 and 5 highlights our main methods (i.e. end-to-end model, experimental setup), and 6 reports our main results. Sections 7 and 8 conclude our paper with a discussion and future works.

2 Background

Task The main goal of fact-checking is to validate the truthfulness of a given claim. Each claim is assigned one of three labels: support, refute, or not enough information (NEI) to verify.

Dataset We use FEVER (Thorne et al., 2018a), a large-scale fact-checking dataset with around 5.4M Wikipedia documents. Claims were generated by extracting sentences from Wikipedia (with possible mutations), and were annotated by humans with their verification label and/or evidence sentences from Wikipedia.

Traditional pipeline Traditional fact-checking systems (Fig. 1a) access knowledge within an external knowledge base (i.e. Wikipedia) to validate a claim. They use a multi-step, pipelined approach, which involve IR-modules, such as document retrievers and evidence selectors, for retrieving the appropriate evidence, and verification modules that take in {`claim, [evidences]`} pairs and predict a final verification label

Our pipeline As shown in Fig.1b, our proposed pipeline replaces both the external knowledge base as well as the IR modules with a pretrained language model. In the remainder of this paper, we utilize BERT. Future work can explore other language models.

Querying the Language Model In Petroni et al. (2019), language models were used as knowledge base to answer open-domain questions. To do this, the authors devised a probe known as "LAMA", which generates fill-in-the-blank cloze-style statements from questions. For example, in order to answer the question 'Where is Microsoft's headquarter?', the question would be rewritten as as 'Microsoft's headquarter is in [MASK]' and fed into a language model for the answer.

Inspired by LAMA (Petroni et al., 2019), we also generate evidences from language models through fill-in-the-blank style tasks.

3 Exploratory Experiments

In order to determine the feasibility of our approach, we began by conducting a human review study on 50 random-selected claims from FEVER (Thorne et al., 2018a). Participants were asked to validate each claim with *only* a language model, by following these steps:

1. Mask a token from the claim, depending on component of the claim we wish to verify:
   Thomas Jefferson founded the University of Virginia after retiring → Thomas Jefferson founded the University of [MASK] after retiring.
   In this example, the user is verifying which university was founded by Thomas Jefferson. Note that the user could alternatively choose to mask *Thomas Jefferson* in order to verify the founder of University of Virginia.
2. Get the top-1 predicted token from the LM. **Top-1 predicted token = Virginia**.
3. If predicted token matches the masked token, the claim is supported, otherwise it is refuted. **Virginia ≡ Virginia → SUPPORTS**

In other words, we asked participants to serve as the "masking" and "verification classifier" components of our fact-checking pipeline in Fig. 1b.

Two participants examined the 50 claims, and eventually achieved an average accuracy of 55%. [1]

We also conducted this zero-shot study on a larger scale and in a more systematic way, by taking all claims in the *full* FEVER dataset, and always masking the last token.[2] Otherwise, we preserve steps 2 and 3 from above. Even with this naïve

[1]Both participants had NLP background, and both were familiar with FEVER and the fact-checking task. We also assumed both participants were capable of selecting the optimal position to mask.

[2]We omit examples for which the masked token is not in BERT's vocab.

token-matching approach, we were able to obtain precision 56% and F1 59% for the positive label (SUPPORT).

Our preliminary experiments' results illustrate that, with a good masking mechanism and verification model, language models can indeed feasibly be used for fact-checking.

4 End-to-End Fact-Checking Model

Enlightened by results from our preliminary experiments, we devise an end-to-end model that automates and improve upon the masking and verification steps that were conducted by humans. Specifically, we resolve two limitations: 1. manual masking of claims, and 2. naïve validation of the predicted token that fails to deal with synonyms and other semantic variants of the answer.

Automatic Masking We mask the *last named entity* in the claim, which we identify using an off-the-shelf Named-Entity-Recognition (NER) model from spaCy Honnibal and Montani (2017). In particular, we choose to mask named entities in order to better ensure that the token we mask actually makes use of the *knowledge* encoded in language models. (Otherwise, we may mask tokens that only make use of the LM's ability to recover linguistic structures and syntax – for instance, masking stopwords). This hinges on the observation that, for most claims, its factuality hinges upon the correctness of its entities (and the possible relations between them), and *not* on how specifically the claim is phrased.

Verification using Entailment To move beyond naïvely matching predicted and gold tokens, we leverage a textual entailment model from AllenNLP (Gardner et al., 2018) to validate our LM predictions. Note that textual entailment models predict the directional truth relation between a text pair (i.e. "sentence *t* entails *h*" if, typically, a human reading *t* would infer that *h* is most likely true).

Full-pipeline steps Detailed steps for our end-to-end model (Fig. 2) are as follows:

1. Masked the last named entity found by the NER model.

2. Get the top-1 predicted token from the LM, and fill in the [MASK] accordingly to create the "evidence" sentence.

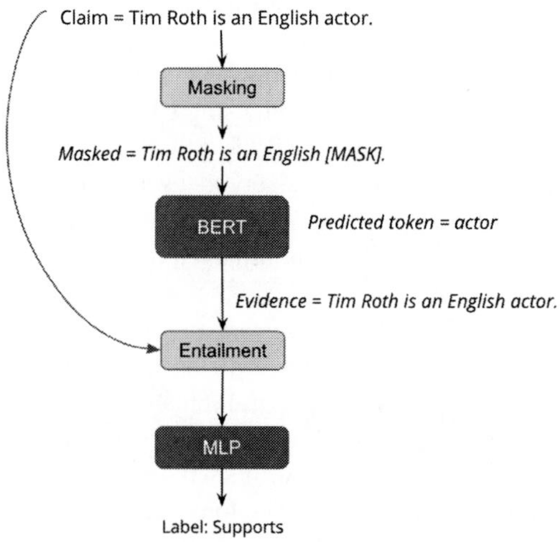

Figure 2: Detailed illustration of our pipeline

3. Using the claim and generated "evidence" sentence, obtain entailment "features" using outputs from the last layer of the pretrained entailment model (before the softmax).

4. Input the entailment features into a multi-layer perceptron (MLP) for final fact-verification prediction.

5 Experiments

5.1 Experiment setup

We conduct our experiments on the FEVER claim verification dataset (Thorne et al., 2018a) using the standard provided splits. We use the publicly available 24-layer BERT-Large as our language model, which was pre-trained on Wikipedia in 2018.[3]

The MLP was optimized using Adam, and trained with a mini-batch size of 32. The learning rate was set to 0.001 with max epoch size 200 and epoch patience of 30. The embedding size of the entailment features (from the pre-trained entailment model) was 400, and our MLP classifier had hidden size of 100.

5.2 Evaluation Metric

The traditional pipeline was evaluated using FEVER scoring, which is a stricter form of scoring that treats predictions to be correct only when correct evidences were retrieved. Since our pipeline

[3]It's possible the model was trained on a later Wikipedia dump than what's released as part of FEVER, but pre-training BERT from scratch is beyond the scope of this paper.

Model	Label	prec	recall	f1	accuracy	macro prec	macro recall	macro f1
	REFUTES	0.36	0.69	0.47				
$BERT_{freeze}$	SUPPORTS	0.43	0.09	0.15	0.38	0.39	0.38	0.33
	NEI	0.39	0.35	0.37				
	REFUTES	0.62	0.55	0.58				
$BERT_{finetune}$	SUPPORTS	0.54	0.67	0.59	0.57	0.57	0.57	0.57
	NEI	0.57	0.49	0.53				
	REFUTES	0.76	0.38	0.51				
$BERTasKB$	SUPPORTS	0.41	0.92	0.57	0.49	0.59	0.49	0.44
	NEI	0.58	0.15	0.24				
SoTA (Thorne et al., 2018b) *	-	-	-	-	**0.68**	-	-	-

Table 1: Performance comparison between BERT-as-encoder models ($BERT_{freeze}$, $BERT_{finetune}$) and BERT-as-LM model ($BERTasKB$) (*We report fact-checking label accuracy, not FEVER score - a stricter form of scoring

does not utilize an external knowledge base, and does not have an evidence retriever, we only examine the correctness of the final verification step using precision, recall, F1 and accuracy. We leave generating evidences with language models for future work.

5.3 Baselines

We introduce two language model baselines for comparison. The first baseline, $BERT_{freeze}$, uses an MLP layer on top of a frozen BERT encoder to make predictions (gradients backpropagate to the MLP layer only). In this baseline, we aim to *extract* the already stored knowledge within BERT model as an embedding vector, and avoid finetuning the internal layers, in order to disentangle BERT's knowledge from it's ability to serve as a high-capacity classifier.

The second baseline, $BERT_{finetune}$, allows all the model layers to be updated based on the fact-verification loss from the MLP layer. This baseline captures BERT's ability as *both* a language model, and a high-capacity text encoder.

Note that the dataset is evenly distributed among the three classes, therefore a random baseline would yield an accuracy of 33%. Also note that the Fever-baseline model introduced by the task organizers achieves accuracy score of 48.8% (Thorne et al., 2018b).

6 Results and Discussion

The results of the three models are reported in Table 1. We observe that our proposed approach ($BERTasKB$) outperforms $BERT_{freeze}$ on all metrics suggesting that querying language models in QA style is a better approach for extracting their encoded knowledge. Similarly, $BERTasKB$ model achieves an accuracy score of 49% which is comparable to Fever-baseline at 48.8%, except without the need for explicit document retrieval and evidence selection. This suggests that language models, used as sources of knowledge for fact checking, are at least as effective as standard baselines. However, there is still much room for future research, as the state-of-the-art model on the Fever shared task achieves an accuracy score of 68.21% (Thorne et al., 2018b).

On the other hand, we find that $BERTasKB$ lags behind $BERT_{finetune}$, as expected, on most metrics. We hypothesize this is due to the high capacity of the model, in comparison, and to the effectiveness of BERT models in text classification. Upon examining the results of these two models closely, we find that $BERTasKB$ struggles mightily with the `NEI` category (F1 score of 0.24 vs 0.53) indicating that our current approach might need specific modules to better tackle that category. As both models seem to be equally adept in identifying the `support` class (0.57 vs 0.59 F1), indicating that $BERTasKB$ is unable to distinguish between `refute` and `NEI` classes. Future work can further investigate techniques to identify these two categories.

Interestingly, the $BERT_{freeze}$ achieves an accuracy score of 38% which is slightly better than a random baseline which achieves 33%.

7 Analysis of Token Prediction Results

In this section, we provide some examples of tokens predicted from BERT to understand the performance of "evidence generation".

First two examples in Table 2 (a, b) are examples with correct fact-check labels from zeroshot setting. When a claim has enough context, and contains rather rare names such as "Sarawak", BERT manages to predict correct tokens.

ID	Claim	Masked Token	Predicted Token	Label
a	Kuching is the capital of [MASK].	Sarawak	Sarawak	SUPPORTS
b	The Beach's director was Danny [MASK].	Boyle	Boyle	SUPPORTS
c	Tim Roth was born in [MASK]	1961	London	SUPPORTS
d	Chile is a [MASK].	country	democracy	SUPPORTS
e	Seohyun [MASK].	sings	Park	SUPPORTS

Table 2: Examples of token predictions from BERT in zeroshot setting. a, b are correctly fact-checked examples, and c, d, f are wrongly fact-checked examples.

We also provide detailed analysis on the error cases to facilitate future work in making further improvements:

- One common form of errors is that, the entity type of token prediction is biased towards the way how the training data was written. For example, sentence c from Table 2 illustrates a common claim structure in FEVER dataset which talks about the birth-year of a person (e.g., Tim Roth). However, 100% of our test samples with such structure always predict city/country (e.g., London). The reason is, in Wikipedia, the birth-years are always written in the following structure "PERSON (born DATE)" (e.g., "Tim Roth (born 14 May 1961)"), and birth city/country written in "PERSON was born in city/country" structure (e.g., "Roth was born in Dulwich, London"). Therefore, to obtain birth-year, the claim had to be written as Tim Roth (born [MASK]) to predict correctly.

- Sentence d is another example that the entity type of token prediction is hard to control. "is a..." is a very general prefix phrase, making it hard for BERT model to correctly predict correct entity type.

- There are lots of short claims in FEVER test set (approx. 1100 samples) which has less than 5 tokens (e.g. sentence e). Since there is very little context, BERT struggles to predict correctly.

One of the the main insight we get from these analysis is that, the way the language model is initially pre-trained, greatly determines the way it should be "queried".

8 Conclusions & Future Work

In this paper, we explored a new fact-checking pipeline that use language models as knowledge bases. Unlike previous pipelines that required dedicated components for document retrieval and sentence scoring, our approach simply translates a given claim into a fill-in-the-blank type query and relies on a BERT language model to generate the "evidence". Our experiment shows that this approach is comparable to the standard baselines on the FEVER dataset, though not enough to beat the state-of-the-art using the traditional pipeline. However, we believe our approach has strong potential for improvement, and future work can explore using stronger models for generating evidences, or improving the way how we mask claims.

In the future, we will investigate sequence-to-sequence language models such as BART (Lewis et al., 2019) or T5 (Raffel et al., 2019), that have recently shown to be effective on generative question-answering (Roberts et al., 2020). Similarly, our proposed approach seem to struggle with correctly identifying NEI cases, and we plan to investigate adding specific modules to deal with NEI. Lastly, we plan to explore new ways of pre-training language models to better store and encode knowledge.

Acknowledgements

We would like to thank Fabio Petroni for the helpful discussion and inspiration.

References

Jacob Devlin, Ming-Wei Chang, Kenton Lee, and Kristina Toutanova. 2018. Bert: Pre-training of deep bidirectional transformers for language understanding. *arXiv preprint arXiv:1810.04805*.

Matt Gardner, Joel Grus, Mark Neumann, Oyvind Tafjord, Pradeep Dasigi, Nelson Liu, Matthew Peters, Michael Schmitz, and Luke Zettlemoyer. 2018. Allennlp: A deep semantic natural language processing platform. *arXiv preprint arXiv:1803.07640*.

Matthew Honnibal and Ines Montani. 2017. spacy 2: Natural language understanding with bloom embeddings, convolutional neural networks and incremental parsing. *To appear*, 7(1).

Mike Lewis, Yinhan Liu, Naman Goyal, Marjan Ghazvininejad, Abdelrahman Mohamed, Omer Levy, Ves Stoyanov, and Luke Zettlemoyer. 2019. Bart: Denoising sequence-to-sequence pre-training for natural language generation, translation, and comprehension. *arXiv preprint arXiv:1910.13461*.

Matthew E Peters, Mark Neumann, Mohit Iyyer, Matt Gardner, Christopher Clark, Kenton Lee, and Luke Zettlemoyer. 2018. Deep contextualized word representations. *arXiv preprint arXiv:1802.05365*.

Fabio Petroni, Tim Rocktäschel, Patrick Lewis, Anton Bakhtin, Yuxiang Wu, Alexander H Miller, and Sebastian Riedel. 2019. Language models as knowledge bases? *arXiv preprint arXiv:1909.01066*.

Alec Radford, Karthik Narasimhan, Tim Salimans, and Ilya Sutskever. 2018. Improving language understanding by generative pre-training. *URL https://s3-us-west-2. amazonaws. com/openai-assets/researchcovers/languageunsupervised/language understanding paper. pdf*.

Alec Radford, Jeffrey Wu, Rewon Child, David Luan, Dario Amodei, and Ilya Sutskever. 2019. Language models are unsupervised multitask learners. *OpenAI Blog*, 1(8):9.

Colin Raffel, Noam Shazeer, Adam Roberts, Katherine Lee, Sharan Narang, Michael Matena, Yanqi Zhou, Wei Li, and Peter J Liu. 2019. Exploring the limits of transfer learning with a unified text-to-text transformer. *arXiv preprint arXiv:1910.10683*.

Adam Roberts, Colin Raffel, and Noam Shazeer. 2020. How much knowledge can you pack into the parameters of a language model? *arXiv preprint arXiv:2002.08910*.

James Thorne, Andreas Vlachos, Christos Christodoulopoulos, and Arpit Mittal. 2018a. Fever: a large-scale dataset for fact extraction and verification. *arXiv preprint arXiv:1803.05355*.

James Thorne, Andreas Vlachos, Oana Cocarascu, Christos Christodoulopoulos, and Arpit Mittal. 2018b. The fact extraction and verification (fever) shared task. *arXiv preprint arXiv:1811.10971*.

Maintaining Quality in FEVER Annotation

Henri Schulte, Julie Binau, Leon Derczynski
IT University of Copenhagen
Denmark
{hens, jubi, ld}@itu.dk

Abstract

We propose two measures for measuring the quality of constructed claims in the FEVER task. Annotating data for this task involves the creation of supporting and refuting claims over a set of evidence. Automatic annotation processes often leave superficial patterns in data, which learning systems can detect instead of performing the underlying task. Humans also can leave these superficial patterns, either voluntarily or involuntarily (due to e.g. fatigue). The two measures introduced attempt to detect the impact of these superficial patterns. One is a new information-theoretic and distributionality based measure, *DCI*; and the other an extension of neural probing work over the ARCT task, *utility*. We demonstrate these measures over a recent major dataset, that from the English FEVER task in 2019.

1 Introduction

The FEVER task frames verification of claims given knowledge as a retrieval and three-class entailment problem. Given a claim, supporting or refuting text must be found, and a judgment made as to whether or not the text supports the claim.

One way in which annotation performance lapses present is with the use of shortcuts. An easy shortcut for this task would be to insert a few direct negation words into claim texts, thus making them clash with the associated evidence. A recent study of ARCT, the Argument Reasoning Comprehension Task, in which systems have to pick a warrant given a claim a premise, found that annotators were prone to inserting words such as 'not' when constructing negative examples, which later models (such as BERT) could then pick up on (Niven and Kao, 2019). These superficial shortcuts were prevalent to the extent that removing this information led to a significant drop in BERT argument reasoning performance, from 77% to 50%.

Mindful of the similar nature of the ARCT and FEVER tasks, we apply an extended version of Niven & Kao's metric to the FEVER dataset, and present an information theoretic measure over skip-grams in FEVER claims to detect candidate superficial features.

2 Annotation in FEVER

The annotation process for FEVER is involved. The FEVER dataset (Thorne et al., 2018) comprises a total of 185,445 claims created from Wikipedia articles and annotated as either `SUPPORTS`, `REFUTES` or `NOTENOUGHINFO`. Additionally, claims that are labelled `SUPPORTS` and `REFUTES` also come with the evidence against which this judgement has been made. This FEVER data was created with the help of 50 annotators and in two stages: First creating claims from Wikipedia articles, then labelling them against evidence from Wikipedia. The claim generation stage entails providing annotators with a randomly sampled sentence from the introductory section of an English Wikipedia article and asking them to create claims about the article's entity. In addition to basing their claims on the provided sentence alone, annotators were also given the choice to utilize information from hyperlinked articles to allow for more complex claims (Thorne et al., 2018). Annotators were also asked to create different variants of these claims by, for example, negating, generalizing or replacing part of the claim. This was done to introduce refutable and non-verifiable claims into the dataset. While trialing, the authors realized that "the majority of annotators had difficulty generating non-trivial negation mutations [...] beyond adding 'not' to the original" (Thorne et al., 2018). We investigate the impact of these trivial negations on the quality of the dataset later on. In the second stage, annotators labeled the previously

Proceedings of the Third Workshop on Fact Extraction and VERification (FEVER), pages 42–46

created claims as either SUPPORTS, REFUTES or NOTENOUGHINFO. For the first two classes, annotators also marked the sentences they used as evidence for their decision. Once again, the annotators had access to articles hyperlinked in the entity's article as well. The final dataset is segmented into multiple subsets, with the training set retaining a majority of the claims at a size of 145,449. The quality of their annotations is ensured by cross-checking labels through five-way agreement, *Super-Annotators* and even validation by the authors themselves. Yet, despite spotting the issue with non-trivial negations early in the process, they do not report on any investigations into the quality of their claims. One might argue that annotation accuracy loses its importance if the task is performed on the basis of biased data. Nevertheless, as with most complex annotation tasks over language, the complex nature of this annotation process is prone to annotation exhaustion and shortcuts (Pustejovsky and Stubbs, 2012).

3 Quality Metrics

We propose two quality metrics for FEVER. The goal of FEVER data is to help train inference/verification/entailment tools that are well-generalised. Thus, a quality metric should help detect when annotated data risks being unsuitable for that purpose. The new metrics outlined here are generic and can be applied to data for other classification tasks. They are proposed with the goal of identifying surface-level linguistic patterns that 'leak' class information, helping dataset builders improve the quality of their data.

3.1 Dataset-weighted Cue Information

The first metric we propose is a simple information theoretic measure of how much a pattern contributes to a classification. In this case, patterns are extracted using skip-grams. These capture a good amount of information about a corpus (Guthrie et al., 2006) while also giving a way of ignoring the typically-rare named entities that are rich in FEVER claims and focusing on the surrounding language. The metric is the weighted inverse information gain of a skip-gram relative to a pair of classes. Weighting is determined by the frequency of documents bearing the skip-gram in the corpus, which normalises skew from highly imbalanced but rare phrases. For dataset D and cue k, where cues are e.g. skip-gram features:

$$IG(D,k) = H(D) - H(D|k) \quad (1)$$

We are interested in items that cause high information gain, i.e. $1 - IG(D, f)$.

This should be weighted with the impact that a pattern can potentially have in a given dataset and split. For this reason, feature counts should be normalised by the size of each class. That is, when calculating entropy:

$$H(X) = -\Sigma_{i=1}^{n} P(x_i) log P(x_i) \quad (2)$$

Let $D_{cue=k}$ be the set of data bearing cue k, and $D_{class=y}$ be the set of data with class label y drawn from the set of class labels Y. The normalised distribution N of cue frequencies for cue k is:

$$N = \{\frac{|D_{cue=k} \cap D_{class=i}|}{|D_{cue=k}|} | i \in Y\} \quad (3)$$

Given this class-balanced dataset weighting, we can then define the information-based factor λ_h trivially thus:

$$\lambda_h = 1 - H(N) \quad (4)$$

A term is also required to correct for the rareness of features. Features that occur only for one class, but are seldom, should not receive a high value. On the other hand, knowing that features in language typically follow a Zipfian frequency distribution (Montemurro, 2001), one should still have useful resolution beyond the most-frequent items. Thus we specify a frequency-based scaling factor λ_f as a root of the scaled frequency weight:

$$\lambda_f = (|d\hat{k} : d \in D||D|^{-1})^{\frac{1}{s}} \quad (5)$$

Where s is a scaling factor corresponding to the estimated exponent of the features' power law frequency distribution. For English, $s = 3$ gives reasonable results (i.e. taking the cube root).

These two are combined taking their squared product to form DCI:

$$DCI = \sqrt{\lambda_h \times \lambda_f} \quad (6)$$

A note regarding language: in this case, we consider 1, 2, and 3-grams, with skips in the range of $[0, 2]$. This is suitable for English; other languages might benefit from broader skip ranges.

3.2 Cue Productivity and Coverage Probes

We follow the approach of Niven and Kao (2019) in determining a productivity and coverage score for each cue in the data. As the structure of their dataset is fundamentally different from the dataset presented in Thorne et al. (2018), we have made amendments to their methodology in order to attain comparable results.

As in Niven and Kao (2019), we consider any uni- or bigram a potential cue. We extract these cues from the claims in the dataset and take note of the associated label. This allows us to calculate the *applicability* of a given cue (α_k), which represents the absolute number of claims in the dataset that contain the cue irrespective of their label. Let $\mathbb{T}$ be the set of all cues and n the number of claims.

$$\alpha_k = \sum_{i=1}^{n} \mathbb{1}\left[\exists k \in \mathbb{T}\right] \tag{7}$$

The *productivity* of a cue (π_k) is the frequency of the most common label across the claims that contain the cue. In practical terms, the productivity is the chance that a model correctly labels a claim by assigning it the most common label of a given cue in the claim.

$$\pi_k = \frac{\max\left[\sum_{i=1}^{n} \mathbb{1}\left[\exists j, k \in \mathbb{T}_j\right]\right]}{\alpha_k} \tag{8}$$

From this definition productivity may be in the range $[\frac{1}{m}, 1]$ where m is the number of unique labels – three in our case. The coverage of a cue (ξ_k) is defined by Niven and Kao (2019) as $\xi_k = \alpha_k/n$. We retain this definition with the caveat that, due to the fundamentally different architecture of the data, we derive α_k differently.

This approach assumes a balanced dataset with regard to the frequency of each label. If executed on an imbalanced dataset, a given cue's productivity would be dominated by the most frequent label, not because it is actually more likely to appear in a claim with that label but purely since the label is more frequent overall. We generate a balanced sample by undersampling majority classes. In order to not discard data from the majority classes, however, we repeat the process ten times with random samples. We find that this is a better compromise than oversampling minority classes or introducing class weights when calculating productivity, as those methods inflate the productivity of rare cues that appear exclusively in the smallest class.

Cue	Productivity	Coverage
a	0.36	0.34
is	0.38	0.32
in	0.37	0.30
the	0.36	0.26
was	0.35	0.25

Table 1: Top five cues by coverage

Cue	Productivity	Coverage
not	0.86	0.04
only	0.90	0.04

Table 2: High-productivity cues

Productivity values alone are not necessarily comparable across datasets. Niven and Kao (2019) acknowledge that a cue is only useful to a machine learning model if $\pi_k > 1/m$. In their case, every claim can have two possible labels, i.e. $m = 2$. For the FEVER dataset three labels exist. This means that the productivity threshold at which cues start becoming useful to a model is higher in the ARCT task. We should therefore actually consider the *utility* of a cue to the model (ρ_k).

$$\rho_k = \pi_k - \frac{1}{m} \tag{9}$$

4 Running the metrics

4.1 Neural Probe Results

We apply the described methodology to the FEVER training dataset presented in Thorne et al. (2018) and thereby determine productivity and coverage for 14,320 cues. Considering the cues with a productivity of 1, i.e. cues that could predict the label with a 100% accuracy, is not particularly relevant as none of them have a coverage over 0.01, meaning that they only appear in $\leq$ 1% of claims. In fact, there are 12,126 cues that only ever appear with one label ($\approx$ 85%).

Table 1 shows the cues with the highest coverage. It is dominated by common English stop words with productivity near the minimum of $\frac{1}{3}$. This means that to a machine learning model these cues provide very little utility in finding a shortcut. Some of the more common cues do still provide some utility though. The cues "an", "to" and "and" each appear in 6-8% of all claims and provide 0.44, 0.53 and 0.49 productivity respectively.

Cue	Utility	Coverage	Harmonic Mean
to	0.19	0.07	0.10
an	0.10	0.08	0.09
and	0.15	0.06	0.09
is	0.04	0.32	0.08
not	0.53	0.04	0.07
only	0.56	0.04	0.07

Table 3: Top seven cues by harmonic mean of utility and coverage

These values pale, however, in comparison to the slightly less common but considerably more productive cues "not" and "only" (see table 2). While these only have a coverage of 0.04 each (Table 2, they provide productivity of 0.86 and 0.90 respectively. Even though Thorne et al. (2018) explicitly mention that they attempted to minimize the use of "not" for the creation of refuted claims, we find that in our sample claims containing "not" were labelled `REFUTES` 86% of the time. We find no other cues with comparable coverage to reach such high productivity.

Niven and Kao (2019) find that in the Argument Reasoning Comprehension Task (ARCT) dataset (Habernal et al., 2018) the cue "not" has a productivity of 61% and coverage of 64%. In the FEVER training data "not" to has a higher productivity but lower coverage.

For "not" this provides a utility value of ≈ 0.11 in ARCT and ≈ 0.53 in the train set of FEVER, meaning that in the FEVER data the cue provides a significantly higher utility to a ML model.

This conclusion is only drawn from the utility alone though. For the sake of comparability across both utility and coverage, we condense these values to one metric by taking their harmonic mean. We choose the harmonic mean as it assigns higher values to cues that are **both** utilisable and covering. For "not" this results in ≈ 0.19 in ARCT and ≈ 0.07 in the FEVER training data.

Considering cues by their harmonic mean of utility and coverage suggests that despite their high productivity, "not" and "only" might not be the most relevant cues in the data, being preceded by common stop words that yet provide noticeable utility (see Table 3).

Besides "not", some relatively neutral, such as "to" and "and", also appear in a somewhat imbalanced manner. In fact, in our samples 53% of claims containing "to" are labelled as `REFUTES`

DCI	Classes	Skipgram
	unigrams	
0.5830	support/refute	only
0.5684	refute/not enough	not
0.4953	support/refute	not
0.4860	refute/not enough	only
0.4564	support/refute	incapable
0.4486	support/not enough	person
	skip-2-bigrams	
0.3278	refute/not enough	('is', 'not')
0.3226	support/refute	('only', '.')
0.3212	refute/not enough	('not', 'a')
0.3103	support/refute	('There', 'a')
0.3100	refute/not enough	('not', '.')
0.3052	support/refute	('only', 'a')
	skip-2-trigrams	
0.2511	refute/not enough	('is', 'not', '.')
0.2503	refute/not enough	('is', 'not', 'a')
0.2488	refute/not enough	('not', 'a', '.')
0.2466	support/refute	('There', 'is', 'a')
0.2396	support/refute	('is', 'not', '.')
0.2347	support/refute	('only', 'a', '.')

Table 4: Highest DCI skip-grams, i.e. most class-informative superficial features, in the English FEVER dataset

and 49% of claims containing "and" are labelled as `SUPPORTS`. These distributions are hard to predict. We therefore encourage analyses of this during dataset construction.

4.2 DCI Results

DCI enables ranking of superficial n-grams. Table 4 presents the most informative superficial patterns in the FEVER data. We can see that "not" plays a prolific role, especially as part of a trigram. This might be what one would expect given the high utility of this word (Table 3). Both support/refute and refute/not-enough-data partitions give the most highly-ranked skip-grams; support/not-enough-data doesn't generate annotation artefacts as frequently.

5 Discussion

Applying productivity, utility and coverage indicates a dearth of the sort of superficial features in FEVER that were present in previous tasks (namely the ARCT dataset). This is somewhat at odds with other work over FEVER. Schuster et al. (2019) find that local mutual information (LMI) reveals some n-grams that are strongly-associated with negative examples, and are able to predict claim veracity based on claims alone. The phrases that Schuster et al. find match those top-ranked by our DCI metric.

We can therefore see that mutual information-based measures (LMI, DCI) find different biases to frequency-associative measures, such as those use to find cues in the ARCT task. It may be worth applying e.g. LMI or DCI to the ARCT data to see if complementary results emerge.

Note that we examine all n- and skip-grams in the dataset, without smoothing. Suntwal et al. (2019) experiment with removing named entities and rare noun-phrases from their dataset when training models. While this is likely to reduce variances in the data representation, enhancing the signal, the goal of this work is to find the strongest signals, and go down from there, rather than remove noise in a "bottom-up" fashion.

This is not the first investigation into biases related to crowdsourcing and human annotation: Belinkov et al. (2019) find patterns in corpora for inference. Sabou et al. (2014) and Bontcheva et al. (2017) discuss best practices in crowdsourcing for corpus creation. Notably, the number of annotations created by a single annotator should be capped strongly, to avoid nuances of a single worker's style disrupting the data significantly – rather, many annotators should contribute to the data. We propose further controlling quality by looking for superficial patterns during the annotation process, and asking annotators to consider re-formulating their input choices if such patterns are present.

6 Conclusion

Annotators are prone to introducing artefacts, certainly in the construction of datasets involving synthesis of claims and counterclaims. This paper presented metrics and an analysis of the English FEVER dataset with three previously-used measures: productivity, coverage and utility; and a new measure, dataset-weighted cue information. We find that the FEVER dataset is somewhat free of superficial artefacts, and present a truncated set of its most-informative (or most distracting) patterns.

Acknowledgments

This research was partly supported by the Danmarks Frie Forskningsfond project Verif-AI.

References

Yonatan Belinkov, Adam Poliak, Stuart M Shieber, Benjamin Van Durme, and Alexander M Rush. 2019. On adversarial removal of hypothesis-only bias in natural language inference. In *Proceedings of the Eighth Joint Conference on Lexical and Computational Semantics (*SEM 2019)*, pages 256–262.

Kalina Bontcheva, Leon Derczynski, and Ian Roberts. 2017. Crowdsourcing named entity recognition and entity linking corpora. In *Handbook of Linguistic Annotation*, pages 875–892. Springer.

David Guthrie, Ben Allison, Wei Liu, Louise Guthrie, and Yorick Wilks. 2006. A closer look at skip-gram modelling. In *LREC*, pages 1222–1225.

Ivan Habernal, Henning Wachsmuth, Iryna Gurevych, and Benno Stein. 2018. The argument reasoning comprehension task: Identification and reconstruction of implicit warrants. In *Proceedings of the Conference of the North American Chapter of the Association for Computational Linguistics*, pages 1930–1940.

Marcelo A Montemurro. 2001. Beyond the zipf–mandelbrot law in quantitative linguistics. *Physica A: Statistical Mechanics and its Applications*, 300(3-4):567–578.

Timothy Niven and Hung-Yu Kao. 2019. Probing neural network comprehension of natural language arguments. In *Proceedings of the 57th Annual Meeting of the Association for Computational Linguistics*, pages 4658–4664.

James Pustejovsky and Amber Stubbs. 2012. *Natural Language Annotation for Machine Learning: A guide to corpus-building for applications.* O'Reilly Media, Inc.

Marta Sabou, Kalina Bontcheva, Leon Derczynski, and Arno Scharl. 2014. Corpus annotation through crowdsourcing: Towards best practice guidelines. In *LREC*, pages 859–866.

Tal Schuster, Darsh Shah, Yun Jie Serene Yeo, Daniel Roberto Filizzola Ortiz, Enrico Santus, and Regina Barzilay. 2019. Towards debiasing fact verification models. In *Proceedings of the Conference on Empirical Methods in Natural Language Processing (EMNLP)*, pages 3410–3416.

Sandeep Suntwal, Mithun Paul, Rebecca Sharp, and Mihai Surdeanu. 2019. On the importance of delexicalization for fact verification. In *Proceedings of the Conference on Empirical Methods in Natural Language Processing (EMNLP)*, pages 3404–3409.

James Thorne, Andreas Vlachos, Christos Christodoulopoulos, and Arpit Mittal. 2018. FEVER: A Large-scale Dataset for Fact Extraction and VERification. In *Proceedings of the Conference of the North American Chapter of the Association for Computational Linguistics*, pages 809–819.

Distilling the Evidence to Augment Fact Verification Models

Beatrice Portelli[1] **Jason Zhao**[2] **Tal Schuster**[2] **Giuseppe Serra**[1] **Enrico Santus**[2,3]

[1] University of Udine [2] CSAIL, MIT
[3] Decision Science and Advanced Analytics for for MAPV & RA, Bayer
portelli.beatrice@spes.uniud.it, jzhao7@mit.edu,
tals@csail.mit.edu, giuseppe.serra@uniud.it, esantus@mit.edu

Abstract

The alarming spread of fake news in social media, together with the impossibility of scaling manual fact verification, motivated the development of natural language processing techniques to automatically verify the veracity of claims. Most approaches perform a claim-evidence classification without providing any insights about why the claim is trustworthy or not. We propose, instead, a model-agnostic framework that consists of two modules: (1) a span extractor, which identifies the crucial information connecting claim and evidence; and (2) a classifier that combines claim, evidence, and the extracted spans to predict the veracity of the claim. We show that the spans are informative for the classifier, improving performance and robustness. Tested on several state-of-the-art models over the FEVER dataset, the enhanced classifiers consistently achieve higher accuracy while also showing reduced sensitivity to artifacts in the claims.

Claim	Susan Sarandon was nominated for five Emmy Awards.
Evidence	**[wiki/Susan_Sarandon]** On television, she is a five-time Emmy Award nominee, including for her guest roles on the sitcoms Friends 2001 and Malcolm in the Middle (2002), and the TV films Bernard and Doris (2007) and You Don't Know Jack (2010).
Label	SUPPORT
Claim	Fantastic Beasts and Where to Find Them was released only in North America on November 18, 2016.
Evidence	**[wiki/Fantastic_Beasts_and_Where_to_Find_Them_(film)]** Fantastic Beasts and Where to Find Them premiered in New York City on 10 November 2016 and was released worldwide on 18 November 2016 in 3D, IMAX 4K Laser and other large format cinemas.
Label	REFUTE
Claim	Ian Brennan is a film screenwriter.
Evidence	**[wiki/Ian_Brennan_(writer)]** Ian Brennan (born April 23, 1978) is a television writer, actor, producer and director.
Label	NOT ENOUGH INFORMATION

Figure 1: Examples of claim-evidence pairs from the FEVER dataset. The evidence spans extracted by our system are underlined and presented in color.

1 Introduction

The increased quantity of information that circulates in social media and on the Web every day, together with the high cost of assessing its veracity, has demanded the application of natural language processing (NLP) techniques to the task of fact verification. In the last years, the NLP community has proposed a large number of datasets and approaches for addressing this task, facing complicated challenges that are still far from being solved.

The task of fact verification can be split into (i) retrieving one or more candidate pieces of evidence; (ii) assessing whether they are either *supporting* or *refuting* a claim, or whether they contains *insufficient* information to state either of the above. In this paper, we mostly focus on the reasoning between the claim and the evidence.

To generate models that work on real world data, fact verification solutions are expected to: (i) perform well not only on synthetic datasets but also in realistic scenarios, where both text form and text content are highly unpredictable; (ii) produce transparent decisions, providing an explanation for their verdict, so that the readers may consider whether trusting them or not.

To address these two requirements, we propose a model-agnostic framework that includes two modules: (i) a span extractor that aims to identify in the evidence the pieces of relevant information that are informative with respect to the claim; (ii) a classifier that uses the claim, evidence and extracted spans to predict whether the evidence is *supporting*, *refuting* or containing *insufficient* information. The spans extracted by the first module are useful to enhance the classifier and inform the user. Humans can in fact exploit the spans to effectively understand why a claim is true or false.

We evaluate our pipeline with three highly performing neural models on the FEVER dataset (Thorne et al., 2018), comparing the uninformed to the informed setting. While this dataset includes

Proceedings of the Third Workshop on Fact Extraction and VERification (FEVER), pages 47–51
July 9, 2020.

ground truth for both evidence retrieval and evidence classification, in this paper we only exploit the latter annotations. Our experiments show that the models informed with the extracted spans consistently achieve higher performance than their uninformed counterparts, demonstrating the usefulness of spans. We also evaluate our models on the challenging SYMMETRIC FEVER dataset (Schuster et al., 2019), which tests system's robustness in absence of FEVER's artifacts. We find the models trained with our pipeline to achieve higher accuracy.

Finally, we assess the quality of the extracted spans as decision rationales to be shown to end-user. Manually examining a subset of outputs shows that 67% of the *support* and 88% of the *refute* spans are well explanatory with respect to the decision, leading to an aggregated score of 75%.

2 Related Work

Fake news detection has recently gained interest in the NLP community. Most of the initial works have focused on style (Feng et al., 2012) and linguistic approaches (Pérez-Rosas and Mihalcea, 2015). Despite the good performance in synthetic datasets, these methods failed when applied to real-world data. New approaches based on fact verification over retrieved evidence have therefore taken the stage in the literature.

Datasets. Several fact verification datasets were developed over the last decade. Vlachos and Riedel (2014) created a dataset which consisted of 221 statements and hyperlinks to pieces of evidence of various formats. Many datasets were created in the following years, with collections of claims of increasing size and various kinds of additional information. Among them Ferreira and Vlachos (2016)'s debunking dataset (300 rumoured claims and 2,595 associated news articles) and Wang (2017)'s LIAR dataset (12,836 short statements labeled for veracity, topic and various metadata on the speaker). In the last years, most systems have been developed over FEVER (Thorne et al., 2018), a large-scale dataset for Fact Extraction and VERification that consists of 185,445 claims and their related evidence, labeled as either supporting, refuting or not containing enough information.

Approaches. There has been a large development since the first approaches for fact verification (Ferreira and Vlachos, 2016; Wang, 2017; Long et al., 2017). To provide a strong baseline for FEVER, Thorne et al. (2018) proposed a pipeline consisting of document and sentence retrieval and a multi-layer perceptron as textual entailment recognizer. More sophisticated models followed. Among them, the Bi-Directional Attention Flow (BiDAF) network (Seo et al., 2016a), originally introduced for machine comprehension, has been recently adapted to the task of fact verification (Tokala et al., 2019). BiDAF combines LSTMs with both a context-to-query and query-to-context attention, to produce a query-aware context representation at multiple hierarchical levels. Nie et al. (2019) introduced the Neural Semantic Matching Networks (NSMNs), which aligns two encoded texts and computes the semantic matching between the aligned representations with LSTMs and used it to earn the first place in the first competitions organized on the FEVER dataset. Soleimani et al. (2019) exploits the contextualized representations of a pre-trained BERT (Devlin et al., 2019) model for both sentence selection and fact verification.

3 Method

Given a claim $C = \{c_1, \ldots, c_n\}$ and a piece of evidence $E = \{e_1, \ldots, e_m\}$, two word sequences of length n and m respectively, the fact verification problem requires to predict the relation $rel = \{(S)\text{upports}, (R)\text{efutes}, (I)\text{nsufficient}\}$ between E and C.

Framework. We propose a pipeline of two modules: a span extractor M_{span} and a classifier $M_{\text{classifier}}$. The goal of $M_{\text{span}}(C, E)$ is to identify polarizing pieces of information $\{e_{i_1}, \ldots, e_{i_N}\}$ in E without which $rel(E, C)$ would be neutral (i.e. C would neither be entailed nor contradicted by E). The identified pieces of information are passed to $M_{\text{classifier}}$, together with C and E, to perform a three-label classification aimed at predicting $rel(E, C)$: $M_{\text{classifier}}(C, E, \{e_{i_1}, \ldots, e_{i_N}\}) = l \in \{S, R, I\}$.

3.1 Span Extractor

We utilize the TokenMasker architecture from Shah et al. (2020) for M_{span}. This masker was developed to identify the minimal group of tokens without which E would be neutral with respect to C. M_{span} is trained by getting feedback from a pretrained neutrality classifier. Shah et al. (2020) use the ESIM model with GloVe embeddings trained on FEVER as a neutrality classifier. We choose to use the RoBERTa model (Liu et al., 2019) in-

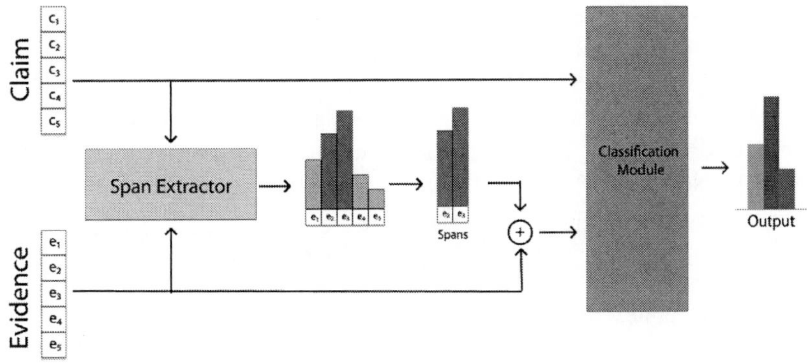

Figure 2: Framework outline: (i) the claim and the evidence pass through the span extractor, which quantifies the relative importance of their words; (ii) claim, evidence and spans are then passed to the classification module, which decides whether the evidence is supporting, refuting or insufficient to judge the claim.

stead, pretrained on an entailment task over a multi-genre corpus (i.e. three-label classification: entailment/neutral/contradiction on the MULTINLI dataset (Williams et al., 2018)).

The choice of using a rationale-style extractor (Shah et al., 2020) is due to its ability to provide informative spans that can be used as explanations to the relation of the evidence with the claim. This approach was shown to perform better than simply relying on the internal attention weights of a classifier (Lei et al., 2016; Jain and Wallace, 2019).

3.2 Classifiers

To test our assumption, we consider three neural network architectures that have achieved the best performance on the first FEVER shared Task recently: BiDAF (Seo et al., 2016b), NSMN (Nie et al., 2019) and BERT (Devlin et al., 2019). Note that the architecture of $M_{\text{classifier}}$ is independent of M_{span}. The spans extracted by $M_{\text{classifier}}$ are forwarded to the classifier by concatenating them to the original evidence, followed by a separator token.

BiDAF consists of four layers: (i) the embedding layer, which encodes two raw text sequences (i.e. C and E) into two vector sequences $\hat{C}$ and $\hat{E}$; (ii) the attention layer, which computes the attention scores between the two sequences and returns two attended sequences C_A and E_A; (iii) the modeling layer, which takes C_A and E_A as input and outputs two fixed size vectors, $\hat{C}_A$ and $\hat{E}_A$, that capture the semantic similarity between the original sequences; and (iv) the output layer, which takes $\hat{C}_A$ and $\hat{E}_A$ and returns the output labels.

NSMN encodes C and E into vector sequences $\hat{C}$ and $\hat{E}$, similarly to BiDAF. It then applies an alignment layer, which computes the alignment matrix, $\mathbf{A} = \hat{C}^T\hat{E}$, and the aligned representations, C_A and E_A, using $\hat{C}, \hat{E}, \mathbf{A}$. It follows a matching layer, which performs semantic matching using LSTM between C_A and $\hat{C}$, as well as E_A and $\hat{E}$, to output matching matrices $\mathbf{M_C}$ and $\mathbf{M_E}$, which are finally pooled by the output layer and mapped to output labels.

BERT (we use the base-uncased version) consists of 12 encoder layers with self-attention $(enc_1, \ldots, enc_{12})$ and one classification layer. Each encoder enc_i takes an input sequence I_{i-1} and outputs I_i, a sequence of the same length where each token is replaced with an embedding capturing its relationship with the other words in I_{i-1}. The output of enc_i becomes the input of enc_{i+1}. I_0 is set as the concatenation of C and E, preceded by the special `[CLS]` token. The output of the last encoder enc_{12} is therefore an highly embedded representation of C and E. It is passed to the classification layer which maps the representation of the `[CLS]` token to the output labels.

4 Experiments

We evaluate the three classifiers described in section 3 in two conditions: uninformed (W/O) and informed (With), where the latter refers to the utilization of the information extracted by M_{span}.

4.1 Data

We use the FEVER dataset to train all of our classifiers. We evaluate the classifiers both on FEVER and on SYMMETRIC FEVER.

FEVER dataset (Thorne et al., 2018): the current

largest available Wikipedia-based dataset, consisting of 185,445 claims. Each claim is matched with supporting or refuting evidence from Wikipedia or with a "not enough information" label.

We use the development set from FEVER's shared-task as our test set (containing 19,998 samples). We randomly split FEVER's training set into our training and validation sets. Following this process, we have 125,451 samples in our training set (73,369 support, 23,109 refute, and 28,973 insufficient information).

While evidence sentences for supporting and refuting examples are provided in the ground truth, those for the "insufficient information" were obtained by us. We use the document retrieval module of the best performing system on the first FEVER Shared Task (Nie et al., 2019). Given a claim and the Wikipedia dump provided with the FEVER dataset, this document retrieval module returns a list of Wikipedia articles which are possibly related to the claim, ranked with a score calculated by comparing the claim, the title of the article and its first sentence. We keep the highest scoring document. Thereafter, we pick the sentence with the highest TF-IDF similarity with the claim. Also, to disambiguate pronouns, we extend all evidence sentences by appending the title of their Wikipedia page.

SYMMETRIC FEVER (Schuster et al., 2019): a smaller unbiased extension of FEVER, consisting of 712 claim-evidence pairs which were synthetically generated from FEVER to remove strong cues in the claims which could allow predicting the label without looking at the evidence (give-away phrases).

4.2 Hyperparameters

TokenMasker is trained on the same dataset and configuration as Shah et al. (2020). However, we replace their neutrailty classifier with a RoBERTa classifier, pretrained on MNLI. This model is trained once and used in inference mode for all subsequent experiments.

BiDAF is trained for 12 epochs using cross entropy loss and Adam optimizer with initial learning rate 1e-3. We use a dropout probability of 0.2 and a batch size of 8.

NSMN is trained for 12 epochs using cross entropy loss and Adam optimizer with initial learning rate 1e-4. We use a dropout probability of 0.5 and a batch size of 8.

BERT is fine-tuned for 8 epochs using cross entropy loss and Adam optimizer with initial learning rate 2e-5. We use a dropout probability of 0.1 and a batch size of 16.

These hyperparemeters were found to achieve the highest accuracy on our validation set. For our final classifiers, we fix these settings and retrain them using the full FEVER training set.

Model	W/O	With	Test set
BiDAF	73.90%	*75.12%	FEVER
NSMN	72.88%	**74.56%	
BERT	84.16%	84.33%	
BiDAF	49.16%	**52.24%	SYMMETRIC
NSMN	53.35%	54.56%	
BERT	71.12%	71.49%	

Table 1: Accuracy of the models on the FEVER and the SYMMETRIC datasets. Results for BERT are the average over 5 runs with the same hyperparameters. Significance: * if $p < 0.1$, ** if $p < 0.05$.

4.3 Results

Table 1 shows the results obtained in our experiments on both FEVER and the SYMMETRIC dataset. Scores are much higher in the first dataset as the systems can rely on give-away phrases, some words in the claims which have a high correlation with the correct output label regardless of the evidence. This situation does not exist in the SYMMETRIC dataset, where the give-away phrases have been eliminated. As expected, all systems perform worse on this dataset, but the drop in performance is more significant for the uninformed models (W/O) than for the informed (With) ones. In fact, the informed models consistently perform better than the uninformed ones (W/O), often obtaining statistical significance. While the difference in performance between W/O and With is particularly relevant for BiDAF and NSMN, it thins for BERT, which is already a strong classifier leveraging on a robust pretraining.

Output Explainability. We also manually evaluated the spans for 100 randomly extracted claim-output pairs, to assess whether they represented an understandable explanation for the verdict. The spans were deemed explanatory in 88% of the cases for *refute* claims and 67% of the *support* claims, which leads to an aggregated score of 75%. The extracted spans are therefore not only informative to the classifier, but can also be used to produce human-readable justifications for a positive or negative relation.

5 Conclusions

This paper has introduced a classifier-agnostic framework that allows fact verification models to improve their performance and robustness, utilizing concise spans of the available evidence sentences. The experiments have shown that the extracted spans are indeed informative for the final classifier, supporting the usefulness of the framework. Furthermore, this work opens the possibility of providing to the human users a justification for the model's predictions.

References

Jacob Devlin, Ming-Wei Chang, Kenton Lee, and Kristina Toutanova. 2019. BERT: Pre-training of deep bidirectional transformers for language understanding. In *In NAACL-HLT*.

Song Feng, Ritwik Banerjee, and Yejin Choi. 2012. Syntactic stylometry for deception detection. In *ACL*.

William Ferreira and Andreas Vlachos. 2016. Emergent: a novel data-set for stance classification. In *HLT-NAACL*.

Sarthak Jain and Byron C. Wallace. 2019. Attention is not explanation. In *NAACL-HLT*.

Tao Lei, Regina Barzilay, and Tommi Jaakkola. 2016. Rationalizing neural predictions. In *Proceedings of the 2016 Conference on Empirical Methods in Natural Language Processing*, pages 107–117, Austin, Texas. Association for Computational Linguistics.

Yinhan Liu, Myle Ott, Naman Goyal, Jingfei Du, Mandar Joshi, Danqi Chen, Omer Levy, Mike Lewis, Luke S. Zettlemoyer, and Veselin Stoyanov. 2019. Roberta: A robustly optimized bert pretraining approach. *ArXiv*, abs/1907.11692.

Yunfei Long, Qin Lu, Rong Xiang, Minglei Li, and Chu-Ren Huang. 2017. Fake news detection through multi-perspective speaker profiles. In *IJCNLP*.

Yixin Nie, Haonan Chen, and Mohit Bansal. 2019. Combining fact extraction and verification with neural semantic matching networks. In *In AAAI*.

Verónica Pérez-Rosas and Rada Mihalcea. 2015. Experiments in open domain deception detection. In *EMNLP*.

Tal Schuster, Darsh Shah, Yun Jie Serene Yeo, Daniel Roberto Filizzola Ortiz, Enrico Santus, and Regina Barzilay. 2019. Towards debiasing fact verification models. In *In EMNLP-IJCNLP*.

Min Joon Seo, Aniruddha Kembhavi, Ali Farhadi, and Hannaneh Hajishirzi. 2016a. Bidirectional attention flow for machine comprehension. *CoRR*, abs/1611.01603.

Minjoon Seo, Aniruddha Kembhavi, Ali Farhadi, and Hannaneh Hajishirzi. 2016b. Bidirectional attention flow for machine comprehension. *ArXiv*, abs/1611.01603.

Darsh J Shah, Tal Schuster, and Regina Barzilay. 2020. Automatic fact-guided sentence modification. In *In AAAI*.

Amir Soleimani, Christof Monz, and Marcel Worring. 2019. Bert for evidence retrieval and claim verification.

James Thorne, Andreas Vlachos, Christos Christodoulopoulos, and Arpit Mittal. 2018. FEVER: a large-scale dataset for fact extraction and verification. In *In NAACL-HLT*.

Santosh Tokala, Vishal G, Avirup Saha, and Niloy Ganguly. 2019. AttentiveChecker: A bi-directional attention flow mechanism for fact verification. In *In NAACL-HLT*.

Andreas Vlachos and Sebastian Riedel. 2014. Fact checking: Task definition and dataset construction. In *LTCSS@ACL*.

William Yang Wang. 2017. "liar, liar pants on fire": A new benchmark dataset for fake news detection. In *ACL*.

Adina Williams, Nikita Nangia, and Samuel Bowman. 2018. A broad-coverage challenge corpus for sentence understanding through inference. In *In NAACL-HLT*.

Author Index

Association for Computational Linguistics
209 N. Eighth Street
Stroudsburg, Pennsylvania 18360

ISBN 978-1-7138-1385-9

CURRAN ASSOCIATES INC.
proceedings.com